Relax,

You Don't Have to

Sell

**How You Can Make Sales Without Being Pushy
... with Authentic Marketing**

from GetTheBigYES.com

Tom Marcoux
Spoken Word Strategist
Executive Coach – Pitch Coach
Speaker-Author of 44 books
CEO

A QuickBreakthrough Publishing Edition

Other Books by Tom Marcoux:

- Soar with Confidence: Pitch – Lead – Succeed
- Dark Arts Defense Against Toxic People
- Darkest Secrets of Charisma
- What the Rich Don't Say about Getting Rich
- Secrets of Awesome Dinner Guests: Walt Disney, Steve Jobs …
- Amazing You … featuring Secrets of Extreme Confidence
- Time Management Secrets the Rich Won't Tell You
- Darkest Secrets of Persuasion and Seduction Masters
- Darkest Secrets of Making a Pitch to the Film / TV Industry

Tom Marcoux

CONTENTS*
* These are highlights. Much more is in this book!

DEDICATION AND ACKNOWLEDGEMENTS
This work is dedicated to YOU. Here are **Special Offers:**

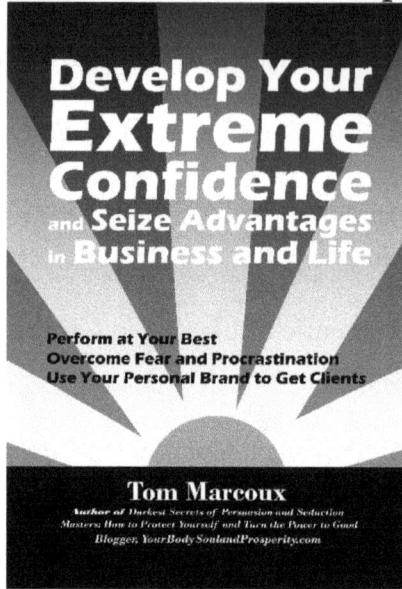

- **Get your free eBook** *Develop Your Extreme Confidence and Seize Advantages in Business and Life* at http://bit.ly/29bVpox
- Apply for a **Free Consultation** with Tom Marcoux https://tomsupercoach.com/breakthrough/

This book also dedicated to the terrific book/film consultant, and author Johanna E. Mac Leod. Thanks to Barry Adamson II for editing a section. Thanks to Johanna E. Mac Leod for this book's cover. Thanks to my father, Al Marcoux, for his concern and efforts for me … and to my mother, Sumiyo Marcoux, a kind, generous soul. Thank you to Higher Power … and to our readers, audiences, clients, my graduate students and my team members of Tom Marcoux Media, LLC and GetTheBigYES.com. The best to you.

Better Than Sales:
How You Can Use Enrolling

"I'm good at what I do, but I hate selling," my client, Alana, said.

"What if I could introduce you to something different? Something that is better than selling and you'll feel good about it," I said.

"Tell me more," she said.

I introduced her to the process of *Enrolling*.

Picture this. You get a prospective client to express what she really wants to accomplish.

In essence, you enroll the person in her highest good.

Then through *Supportive Listening*, your next words truly **resonate** with the person and they want what you offer. The person feels that what you're saying is **relevant**.

This is a whole new paradigm. Gone are the days of standard selling and "overcoming resistance" or "overwhelming the resistance you get."

In this new paradigm, you're *dropping* any methods that include being pushy.

When mentors taught me these methods (and I innovated my own methods), I got excited. Why? Because I felt *free* of trying to push or convince the prospective client of anything.

Let's face it. We don't like people who push their ideas and their so-called logic on us.

Instead, you learn to practice enrolling. You gain clients and feel great doing the process.

My friend, you open a new world when you learn how to enroll people.

And this is when you can *Relax, You Don't Have to Sell.*

Why Many of Us Fail to Do Our Sales Tasks— and How You Can Do Something Better Than Selling

One day as I was walking, a sudden insight arose in my thoughts:

Selling is imposition.
Enrolling is invitation.

No wonder that many of us don't like selling! I'll ask you: Do you like pushing and trying to convince people? You probably have had some unpleasant experiences with unskillful, troublesome salespeople. **You probably want nothing to do with the stereotype of a pushy salesperson— right?**

I suggest that this imposition-type of efforts is old, standard selling.

Instead, **this book will serve you as a breath of fresh air**. I'm excited to share this material with you. After writing two previous books on marketing, I'm thrilled to share with you *my best, recent insights and methods.*

Certain insights provide the power of this book:

Don't sell—Help. – Darren Hardy

"There is no way to happiness. Happiness is the way."
– Dr. Wayne Dyer

You might be curious as to why I included the quote about *happiness is the way.*

The truth I've observed in clients is that it does NOT work to try to become a different person—a "salesperson"—if you find traditional sales to be repulsive.

For *happiness is the way* to be your truthful way of living, you need something *better* than sales. It's called *Enrolling.* (I'll explain that soon.) The truth is: You'll do better if you're *happy* in the way you gain clients.

Additionally, I've helped hundreds of clients and audience members *free themselves* from the antiquated sales methods. They've learned and used top level communication skills to raise their level of success. Enrolling is a level beyond the traditional sales communication patterns.

Don't be a salesperson.
Be an Enroller.

You can feel great in how you gain clients and customers. How? It's about staying true to your core values and communicating in ways that inspire people to trust you.

As I trained MBA students at Stanford University, I guided them in how to communicate powerfully. **The essence of effective communication is congruence.**

Everything must match up: who you are, your product, what the clients need, and your core values.

Why? People are watching for hype, lies, your doubt and more. They seek to first protect themselves.

This is understandable, right?

As an Executive Coach, some of my work is about helping people get out of their own way.

I noticed that before working with me, people procrastinated on doing what's necessary for them to sell their products or services. What was going on?

As I noted before: Many of us do *not* want to become another person—a "salesperson."

The good news is: You can stay the positive person and *avoid* putting on the "façade of a salesperson."

It's all about Enrolling.

What is Enrolling—and How Does This Connect with Authentic Marketing?

Certain definitions of "enroll" seize my attention. These include: a) to take in as a member and b) to become a member.

When I think of "to become a member," I focus on:

- You become one of us
- I become part of you

Think about it. **We can enroll or become part of a movement.**

Here's an example of a movement. Women took direct action toward gaining the vote in the United States. Sometimes, we don't think about it, but for 144 years, women did *not* have the opportunity to vote in the United States.

Women created their own movement and worked for 72 years until women were granted their right to vote in the USA. The 19th Amendment to the U.S. Constitution was ratified by the states on August 18, 1920.

The movement is often cited as beginning in 1848 when Elizabeth Cady Stanton and Lucretia Mott held a convention for women's rights in Seneca Falls, New York.

I shared the above example to illustrate:

- People get excited by a cause
- Progress does happen

Here are three vital parts of Enrolling:

- Don't sell—help
- You become a member of a cause—to help the person you're talking with.
- The person becomes a member of a cause—to use your product/service to *rise up* in her own life

By "rise up," I mean: To elevate to a higher level of living: more success, fulfillment and, perhaps, joy.

This mention of success, fulfillment and joy leads us to talking about Authentic Marketing.

Use Authentic Marketing to Empower Yourself and Your Client

In an article posted at Forbes.com, Young Entrepreneur Council shared this point of view:

"Authentic marketing begins not with tactics or strategy, but with the self. It asks, What do *we* (as an organization) believe? If 'success' is the progressive realization of a worthy ideal, then what ideal or set of ideals do we want to be known for? Other than the commodity that we deliver to our customers, how will we deliver those ideals? ... Authentic marketing comes from your company's sincerely held philosophy; some call this core values. Actions or ideas in disagreement with those values are forced out like antibodies ejecting a virus. This is because the philosophy is one that the organization has decided it will never compromise on."

From the above comment, we note that *core values* are a great place to start the Authentic Marketing process.

What can be a company's core values?

Here's an example: Disneyland

Around 1965, Van France, at Disneyland, created a set of standards that would help *Cast Members* (Disney's term for their employees) create happiness for *Guests* (Disney's term for customers).

Van France identified:

- Safety
- Courtesy
- Show
- Capacity (later identified as "Efficiency")

Let's get specific. Related to "Show," Cast Members devote efforts to maintain the illusion of a particular land. You do *not* see a Cast Member in an astronaut's suit walk through Frontierland.

How about "Efficiency"? In recent years, Disney has innovated the Fast Pass which is a system that gives the Guests a specific time to arrive at an attraction. This system cuts down on crowding and wait times. That certainly increases the Guests' happiness.

Pause Now: What are your Core Values?

For many of us, this can be a daunting question.

With my clients, I came up with a question that cuts through a lot of distractions.

I ask:

How do you heal a part of you as you heal them (target market)?

In some cases, you can ask a doctor: How did you become a doctor?

One doctor says, "A doctor helped me when, as a kid, I broke my arm. I wanted to help people heal up, too."

Here's another approach to the Core Values question. My own values include: Love, Freedom, Creativity, Contribution.

I translated these values into two things:

I help people experience enthusiasm, love and wisdom to fulfill Big Dreams. – Tom Marcoux's Personal Mission

We create energizing, encouraging edutainment for our good and humankind's rise. – Tom Marcoux Media, LLC Company Mission

Exercise 1: Quickly, with no hesitation, write down eight values that mean something to you personally.

Now, circle your top four values.

To get the most from this book, write down your responses to the various exercises in a personal journal.

Jotting things down for even 20 seconds provides you with more value than merely reading.

Enrolling #1

How to Go from Your Values to Serving Your Clients

In this section, we'll look at two processes:

1) Develop Your Values-to-Message Progression
2) Keep Free of Hype and Stay with Authentic Marketing

1. Develop Your Values-to-Message Progression

I have developed a process in which my clients go from a personal value all the way through to an authentic marketing message.

Here's the Values-to-Message Progression

One of Your Personal Values → Service You Offer → Prospective Client's Need/Values → Attention-Grabbing Authentic Message to Seize Person's Attention

Here's an example:
Personal Value: Mindy wants to be free of money worries.

Service She Offers: She helps people design an online course. (She teaches this through her own online course.)

Prospective Clients Need/values: Express creativity and gain financial abundance.

Attention Grabbing Authentic Message to Seize Person's Attention:

A rough draft of the message:
Want to do work one time and gain a continual stream of income?

Want to have no ceiling on your money gaining opportunities?

Now, it's your turn
Exercise #2: Express Your "Values-to-Message
Progression":
One of Your Personal Values → Service You Offer → Prospective Clients' Needs/Values → Attention-Grabbing Authentic Message to Seize Person's Attention

Go to the next page to Use the *Values-to-Message Progression* Form:

Values-to-Message Progression **Form**

One of Your Personal Values	
Service You Offer	
Prospective Clients' Needs/Values:	
Attention Grabbing Authentic Message to Seize Person's Attention	
Rough Draft for Your Message	

© Tom Marcoux Media, LLC   GetTheBigYES.com

* * * * * *

2) Keep Free of Hype and Stay with Authentic Marketing

Definitions of hype include: "to promote or publicize extravagantly" and "deception."

An Example of the Difference between "Hype Marketing" and "Authentic Marketing"

I've worked with several software engineers in Silicon Valley, California. One thing I've noticed is their huge dislike of "hype."

Years ago, I saw this advertising phrase: "The only sales book you'll ever need."

I find this promise or "hype" to be overreaching. Why? I've studied several books on sales, persuasion, prospecting for clients, marketing and more. No one book was enough.

And, I learned much from all the books I've studied.

Make Sure That You as a Service Provider or Your Product *Lives Up* to a "Big Claim"

Am I saying that you never can make a big claim? No. In fact, in the noisy environment of the various forms of media, you may need to *say something vivid and loud*. That is NOT the same as making essentially a false claim. To me "the only sales book you'll ever need" is such a false claim.

A Big Claim might be: "You'll feel better as you shift from selling to the new paradigm of Enrolling."

Can you be sure that the person listening to your speech or watching your video will have such an experience? No. However, you can observe such a change in feeling in yourself and in your clients.

If you use a Money Back Guarantee, you can return the fee for your product to the occasional person who is *the exception.*

Here we're looking at the distinction between a "hype message" and a "Big Claim message."

To say, "You'll never need to read another sales book" is hype. We cannot know that.

On the other hand, to say "You'll feel better as you shift from selling to the new paradigm of Enrolling" is based on *evidence that you have seen in yourself and your clients.*

Nothing works for everyone.

However, over time, we can observe human behavior and invite people to comment on their experiences with our products/services. **With such evidence, we can craft a compelling message.**

Next, we'll discuss the role of Authentic Marketing in creating a compelling message.

Exercise #3: Write down your own three versions of a claim:

a) *Hype* version
   (example: "The only sales book you'll ever need")

b) *Authentic Marketing* version
   (example: "This book guides you to make real and warm connections that lead to closed sales.")

c) *Big Claim Backed by Evidence* version
   (example: Hundreds of clients and audience members have learned these methods, applied them and improved their sales numbers.)

Tom Marcoux

Enrolling #2

How to Include Authentic Marketing in Creating Your Compelling Message

Authentic marketing begins not with tactics or strategy, but with the self. – Fabienne Frederickson

Blog writer Lizzie Davey wrote:
"[Authentic Marketing is] the process of open communication and being on the 'same page' as the audience you're 'talking' to. It's the notion of creating a dialogue between your brand and your audience that's natural and genuine."

Lizzie Davey noted that one would "create content that reflects your company's personality and your soul."
She also shared these vital elements:

"1. User Generated Content (UGC)
2. Instant Content

3. Customer Stories and Case Studies

Additional Methods:
a) Engage your customers
b) Consider what you audiences need and want
c) Be human
d) Be truthful and transparent
e) Don't promote
f) Put your customers first"

At this point, I want to note two things about creating a compelling message:
1) Focus on customer stories and case studies ("The Telling Quote")
2) Live up to Your Branding

1. Focus on customer stories and case studies ("The Telling Quote")

Let's face this together. Your prospective clients want *results.* What is the clearest expression of the results you achieve? Customer testimonials.

Consider looking for what I call "The Telling Quote." This idea is built upon the fiction-writing pattern of providing the "telling detail." One small detail can have great power in a story.

Similarly, in your Authentic Marketing, you can find a powerful quote that brings home to your prospective clients the great value and results you achieve for your clients/customers.

Here are examples:
- "Tom Marcoux coached me to get more done in 10 days than other coaches in 2 years," – Brad Carlson, CEO

- "Using one of Tom Marcoux's methods, I got more done in 2 weeks than in 6 months." – Jaclyn Freitas, M.A.

Exercise #4: Write down three examples of results that you have achieved with your clients. For each example, write down a quote that the happy client gave you. (Recall any praise the client gave you, perhaps, in an email message.)

2. Live up to Your Branding

Years ago, during a television appearance as a guest expert, I turned to the TV host, who asked me, "How can the viewers find you?"

"TomMarcoux.com," I replied.

"How do you spell Marcoux?" the TV host asked.

That's when I knew I had a problem with my marketing.

I went back to my team and said, "We have a problem."

After a discussion, a new domain was proposed: TomSuperCoach.com

I immediately got the feeling that people in my industry were going to tease me about this. (They have.)

But then I had the full resolve to live up to the term "TomSuperCoach."

I've trained with mentors. I've attended classes and workshops. I keep up and read up to 88 books each year.

I've also learned about what it means to be an expert.

Some years ago, author Bob Bly wrote about what it means to be an expert. I reflected on his comments. Then, I composed this sentence: **"An expert has a system that people like and use."**

So, the website TomSuperCoach.com is *not* hype.

Authentic Marketing includes the pattern that you live up to your own branding. You fulfill whatever promises your branding implies.

Exercise #5: Write down your answers to:

How can you live up to your own branding? What kind of continual training and learning can you make sure you receive? Can you develop "a system that people like and use"?

Special Element of Creating a Compelling Message: Use an *Effective Story*

How do You Avoid Resistance? Tell an Effective Story!

"What are you talking about? I tell stories every day to potential clients," Amy, an audience member asked.

"How that's going for you?"

"You mean, how many sales do I make?" she asked.

"That's an important measurement," I replied.

"Not so well," Amy said, and then she sighed.

The crucial distinction that I brought to Amy's attention is that we must up our game. I have developed a process to enrich your story so you seize the audience's (target market's) attention. You can't just tell a story; you must prepare a professional-level Effective Story.

We'll use the S.T.O.R.Y. process:

S – set how we like the hero

T – target the hero's goal

O – open with a grabber

R – reveal the struggle

Y – yearn for the Triumphant Ending and "What I learned…"

Here I'll share a story that I use in my workshops:

> "People walking on the ocean floor. Bubbles rising up from their helmets. Fish fluttering around the people. That's the image I saw on a TV screen. I was 8 years old—when I saw a feature film, 20,000 Leagues Under the Sea.
>
> Wow! I want to do that!
>
> I held that dream for over forty years.
>
> Then, I found out that I could do helmet diving at the Grand Cayman Island.
>
> Yes!
>
> But then I got scared.
>
> Because when I had to have an MRI Exam, I found out about a big problem that would end my dream.
>
> They stuck me into the MRI machine. It's like being put on a shelf and shoved into the wall. With only 1 inch and half over my nose.
>
> Before the exam, they had a form. Do you have claustrophobia?
>
> I don't know.
>
> Now, in the MRI machine—Yes! Yes! I have claustrophobia!
>
> I even kicked off a cover they had on my legs. I felt SUFFOCATED.
>
> So, here's the big problem that's going to end my dream of walking on the ocean floor.
>
> The diving helmet will trigger my claustrophobia.
>
> How do I know that?
>
> Well—thanks to James Cameron. He directed a feature

film called *The Abyss.*

In that film, you see the world from inside a diving helmet.

Aggh! So small. Can't breathe!

But wait a minute. I have a dream. A dream I've held since I was 8 years old.

I will *not* give up.

Can you relate to that? You have a dream. Many of us here in this room are entrepreneurs. We have a dream. You want to make something. You want to bring it into the world.

What do you need? Strategy.

So, I figured out a strategy so I would not lose my dream of walking on the ocean floor.

I put on a hoodie [sweatshirt] and I practiced. I rehearsed walking on the ocean floor just concentrating on looking forward. I would consciously ignore the helmet. Or hoodie during my rehearsals.

Did it work?

Yes! I walked on the ocean floor.

My big dream came true. The 8-year-old boy in my heart said, YES!

And, fortunately, we're talking about Authentic Marketing in this workshop.

I'm going to work with you on Strategy.

Strategy will make your dreams come true.

You want more clients.

We're going to work on strategy today.

I'll share with your specific methods. And you're going to rehearse and work in what I call Teams of Three.

Each person will have an instant little audience of two colleagues . . ."

I'll now briefly break down the elements of the *Effective Story.*

1. Set how we like the hero

We begin with a little boy and big dream. We like a character with a dream. Many of us will root for the little boy. We see how the character grows up and has trouble and pain—the claustrophobia attack. We relate to characters who endure pain and difficulty. Audiences appreciation such characters known as underdogs.

2. Target the hero's goal

The goal is set from the beginning: "I want to walk on the ocean floor."

3. Open with a grabber

We begin with an interesting image: people walking on the ocean floor. Even better, we begin with a little boy's dream.

4. Reveal the struggle

Audiences (target markets) identify with people who struggle. The main character does not start off as a hero. It's only by using something that person becomes a hero. That something, in your story, it could be your product.

5. Yearn for the Triumphant Ending and "What I learned..."

Let's face it: People like to win and to succeed. When the main character succeeds the audience has the vicarious experience of succeeding, too.

When it comes to using a story in getting a client, be sure

to craft the ending of the story to emphasize the value the previous client gained with your product or service. Part of the Triumphant Ending can be: "That's when Sarah turned to me and said, 'Sam, I'm so glad I hired you! I can always count on you to help me double my sales.'"

I use the phrase *"What I learned..."* as a reminder to include "the moral of the story." In the above example, the previous client "Sarah" learned something: "I can always count on [Sam] to help me double my sales."

In summary, carefully craft your stories for your video marketing or your in-person speeches. Effective stories create more sales.

Exercise #6: Write a rough draft of an Effective Story to use as part of your Authentic Marketing process.

Enrolling #3

Focus on the Big Benefits Your Clients Want and Realize That They Do *Not* Care About Your "Process"

"So, what do you do for your clients?" I asked my client, Alexandra.

"I guide them through a series of meditations that...," Alexandra went on for a while.

"What do they get from that?" I asked.

"What?"

"What are the results? What do they experience? How is their life improved or enhanced?"

"They become relaxed."

"Good. And when they're relaxed, what do they get?"

"I don't understand," she said.

"That's okay. We're exploring here. So, your client is relaxed, what does your client get?"

"Clearer thinking?"

"Are you asking me or telling me?" I asked.

"Oh, yeah. It's true. My client experiences clearer thinking."

"Sounds good. What does your client do with clearer thinking?" I asked.

"My client makes better decisions."

"With better decisions, what does your client get?"

Alexandra paused. She closed her eyes for a moment. Then she smiled. "My client gets financial abundance."

"Tell me more."

"With clearer thinking, not hampered by fear, my client makes better decisions that open the floodgates of financial abundance for her business," Alexandra said.

"Now, we're *'seeing the diamonds,'*" I said. In an extended discussion, I shared with Alexandra three distinctions.

- Your clients want what they want, and they do *not* care about your process
- Your clients are attracted to "shiny objects" or "diamonds"
- "Diamonds" sparkle and stand out from the all the noise in the media and more

During the conversation, I shared my phrase: **To stand out, find out what you stand for.**

"Alexandra, what do you stand for?"

"In life?"

"Yes. And, what do you stand for, in terms of helping your clients?"

"I want them to have financial abundance."

"What will they have then?"

"Peace … inner peace. They won't be so worried about money."

"I hear you, Alexandra. Are *you* worried about money?"

"Yes!"

"So, you want to give your clients what you would like for yourself?"

"I—yes. Is that weird? Is that wrong?"

"It's all good," I said.

Earlier in this book, I shared a question that I often bring into my coaching sessions: "How do you heal part of you as you heal them? ["Them" refers to your target market.]

We've just seen Alexandra's journey to the *Big Benefits:* Inner Peace and Freedom from Money Worries.

Now, Alexandra could focus on *the essence* of the messages in her Authentic Marketing.

Now, I'll share some **examples of Big Benefits:**

- Stop self-sabotage
- Relaxed
- Ease
- More energy
- Stop being so fearful
- Have the success you deserve
- More money
- More time off

To help Alexandra think in terms of Big Benefits, I also explained my process for naming one of my speeches.

I shared with Alexandra: "People don't want time management. They want to get it done, get stronger and get credit for it. So that's how I titled my speech:

Get It Done
Get Stronger
Get Credit for It
—Power Time Management

Time management is a process. People do *not* want a

process. Talking about your process often provides distractions.

Focus on the Big Benefits.

For decades, in journalism, a well-known phrase has been "If it bleeds, it leads." That may seem crude. Still, it does point to what works. People pay attention to blood, disaster, pain, and trouble.

Often, the detail that gets a prospective client to hire you (or your product) is …

Relief from pain.

OR

Relief from anticipated pain. (This is connected to worries like money worries.)

Do not hide the Big Benefits.

If Alexandra talks too much about her process (a series of customized meditations), she will miss the opportunities to get the prospective clients to imagine the freedom and peace they will enjoy when they're released from fear and their limiting beliefs.

Now it's your turn. Focus on Big Benefits.

Exercise #7: Use the Progression of *Heal a Part of Me to Big Benefits* Form.

See the Form on the next page:

Heal a Part of Me to Big Benefits **Progression Form**

Some problem you needed to solve or a part of you that needed healing	
Service You Offer	
How your service heals your clients in some way.	
Identify Big Benefits that your clients enjoy	
Rough Draft of your Marketing Message	

© Tom Marcoux Media, LLC   GetTheBigYES.com

Tom Marcoux

Enrolling #4

How to Create and Refine Your Message

"What do you mean by refine my message?" my client Alex asked.

"Here are two valuable elements: Your message becomes compelling, and you enjoy expressing it," I replied.

Why would you enjoy expressing your authentic marketing message? *Because it is heartfelt. This is crucial for Heart-Centered Business Owners.*

Making Your Message Compelling

When working with a client, especially one who wants to use video marketing, I ask them to consider opening a video with a **Question that Touches Their Pain**. I'm referring to the target market's pain.

This *Question that Touches Their Pain* **can be one possible** *place to begin the creation* **of your marketing message.**

For example, I begin a video to promote my Authentic Marketing workshop with a Question That Touches Their Pain, which is: "Do you need more clients, but somehow every week, you fail to complete your marketing?"

On Facebook, here was a response to this video: "Tom, that is a great message. Clear and structured, taking us on a journey. I hear so many videos of people selling that lack enthusiasm, a clear message, and they are boring. There are a lot of coaches who could definitely learn from attending your presentation. Thank you for your informative and entertaining video."

Script of Tom Marcoux's Authentic Marketing 3-minute Video:

"Do you need more clients but somehow every week you fail to complete your marketing?

Does standard selling turn you off and you want something better?

I'm Tom Marcoux, and I welcome you to Authentic Marketing, the workshop. I'm going to share with you something better than standard selling. We have arrived at a new time.

Something is better, and it's called *Enrolling*. There is something I want to share with you *before this video is done*: The Essence of Enrolling.

Realize that now you can connect with people in an authentic way. You don't have to push in fact you might be a person who doesn't like selling because you've encountered these people push and they try to convince and they try to shove their logic at you. No, you won't be doing any of that because you'll learn how to do *Supportive Listening*. And you will connect with people. You will connect with their vision

---

of what's possible. And you will show them and provide a vision of how, when they get involved with your product or your service, they will rise up in their own life. And they'll find that compelling. And they'll want to buy your product or engage you for your service.

This is exciting and here's the *Essence of Enrolling*. Three words: *Don't sell—Help.* Let me share that again: *Don't sell—Help.*

You can do that right from the start when you use Authentic Marketing now.

Depending on the venue this is in-person as a workshop or online. You'll want to check out the information below to see where and when this workshop is happening for you.

And I am so excited. I will help you especially with your video marketing because of my training as a feature film director, as an actor, and as a screenwriter. I'll help you make things compelling so that people will trust you and so that you will feel great about your Authentic Marketing.

(Video testimonials follow)

Woman: "I really enjoy the way he engaged everybody in all this from the very beginning to the end."

Man: "So, I think this was one of the most fun and interactive sessions we had at Igniters. And some of the tips we got like if you are a speaker or if you are pitching or if you're anywhere close to a stage, and you need to know these things. You need to know all these formulas—all these tricks and tips."

2nd Man: "I love most about Tom's presentation is when he talked about narrative. He talked about the power of a narrative. And what I took away from it is that you shouldn't be telling your audience how to feel. You should be telling them a story and getting them to come to that conclusion themselves."

2nd Woman: "It was very interesting to have these little groups where you work on the concepts together and work on things immediately."

3rd Man: "Overall his energy was great. His examples really caught the audience's attention. It was a great speech. Thanks Tom."

Tom: Attend the workshop. I look forward to working with you. I'm Tom Marcoux. Thank you.

Three Elements of Making Your Marketing Message Compelling

At this point, I'll discuss three vital elements:

1) Use a Question That Touches Their Pain
2) Use "Discovery"
3) Use Video Testimonials

1) Use a Question That Touches Their Pain

Be sure to use the first seconds of your video well. Sometimes, I get amazed at how people waste the first seconds with a filmed montage or "Hi, I'm Joe SomeGuy, and I do ___." Instead, use a Question That Touches Their Pain. As you saw in the above transcript of my video, I begin with "Do you need more clients, but somehow every week, you don't complete your marketing?"

Exercise #8: Write down three alternative versions of a *Question that Touches Their Pain* ("Their" refers to your target market).

2) Use "Discovery"

Do something better than conveying a standard story. Instead, catch the viewers' attention. In the above video, I say, "Before the end of this video, I'll share with you the Essence of Enrolling." This is a promise that the viewer will *discover* something new and helpful.

Exercise #9: Write down three alternative versions of some "secret" you can share before the end of your video.

3) Use Video Testimonials

Real power is found in hearing and watching testimonials.

How does any video viewer know that you're good at what you're offering?

The proof becomes clear in the positive comments of happy clients.

After a workshop, people line up to talk with me. After I've listened well and offered some guidance (requested by the person), I then ask, "Did you get value from the workshop?"

The person starts to share their favorite part of the workshop, and I say, "Oh, would you share a couple of words for a video on my smartphone?"

That's when I hold up my smartphone.

99% of the time, the person says, "Yes!"

Then I ask them to place the microphone on their lapel, and they give me a video testimonial.

After they express themselves, I ask, "Would you say your name, please?"

The above sequence features a wise order.

You ask for the person's name after they have spoken. This prevents the person from becoming self-conscious.

It all feels casual.

Still, the video testimonials are worth so much for increasing your circle of clients!

Exercise #10: Rehearse asking for a testimonial and then filming one with your smartphone—with a couple of your friends.

Enrolling #5

The *Enrolling Process* via an In-person Conversation with a Prospective Client

"Wow!" my client, Sarah, began. "I just got a new client. And it didn't feel like selling. I felt like I was helping the person from the beginning of the phone call."

That's the experience of Enrolling.

The Essence of Enrolling is *Don't Sell — Help.*

Earlier, I shared my comment:

Selling is imposition.
Enrolling is invitation.

What do we invite the prospective client to do? Here are **Three Invitations:**

Let's Explore ...

1) Your Vision ("The Vision for Your Best Life" ... *The Emerald City*)
2) Your Current Situation (Often, this includes pain and *"The Weeds"*)
3) How we might work together to fulfill Your Vision

The metaphor that I often use is: "The person wants to *Live in The Emerald City*, but they're stuck in *The Weeds*."

I'll first discuss this process in the context of a "free strategy session" — that you conduct on the telephone. Later, in this section, I will talk about how the principles apply when you use video marketing.

How to Get the Person to Welcome Your Phone Call

Later in this book, I talk about giving a speech to a group and then having audience members apply for a limited amount of free consultations that you offer. You use the application as a method to identify only the best prospective clients.

(With the people who are *not* a match, you send them a free eBook. They got something for their effort to apply for your limited number of free consultations).

[For more information about this process, see the section *"... speaking to a group and accepting applications for a free consultation."*]

As part of the beginning of the Free Strategy Session phone call, you present an Agenda. This can sound like:

"I've done many of these strategy sessions, and it helps to have an agenda.

"So, we have three main parts.

"First, we'll talk about your vision. About what you really want for your business and your life.

"Second, we'll talk about your current situation.

"And third, if and only if we have a match, we can talk about how we might work together.

"That sound good, [person's first name]?"

You note how I end my above paragraph with a question. One of my mentors said, "Ask people for permission, when appropriate. Keep the person engaged. For example, before launching into a story, you could ask, 'Would you like to hear how one of my clients faced a similar situation and …?'"

So, my friend, are you ready to explore the Three Invitations in more detail?

Great!

The Three Invitations

Let's explore:

1) Your Vision ("The Vision for Your Best Life" … *The Emerald City*)
2) Your Current Situation (Often, this includes pain and *"The Weeds"*)
3) How we might work together to fulfill Your Vision

1. Let's Explore Your Vision ("The Vision for Your Best Life" … *The Emerald City*)

How you approach this material depends on the prospective client. Sometimes, I use my metaphor of *The Emerald City*. This represents what the person truly wants:

comfort, success, joy and confidence.

Recently, I was coaching Mark, a client, and I said, "You need to do a lot of *Supportive Listening*."

"Tell me more about Supportive Listening. I'm not exactly sure how all this fits together," he said.

"Here's a way to look at it. ***Enrolling is about joining a cause. Until you do Supportive Listening, you do not know what the person's cause is.***"

Specifically, people are different, and they have a different order of their personal values (related to The Emerald City) of *comfort, success, joy and confidence.*

You can find out—through Supportive Listening—what the person values the most.

A Brief Overview of Supportive Listening

Your focus-points are:

- Help the person experience their own thoughts and feelings
- Listen to understand and feel what is most important to the other person
- Keep the spotlight on the other person (***avoid*** trying to sell the person something and ***avoid*** trying to convince the person of anything
- Help the person feel that they are ***being heard*** by you

The experience of Being Heard is so important that I wrote a book on the topic, *Be Heard and Be Trusted.*

Here are examples of questions one can use in the process of "Let's Explore Your Vision":

- So, tell me about your great future. What are you going to experience with your business when everything goes right in the future?

- When you have _____, then what do you get?
- How does it feel when you've reached _____?
- What will be a great thing about each day once you've reached _____?
- What new and enjoyable thing are part of your life? [You notice that this question shifts the person *into* the future.]
- Do you have some thoughts and feelings about what might be your legacy?
- What do you want the most?
- How will you feel when you have it?
- What feels so great as you're now doing what you really want to do?
- When you say _____, I feel your excitement. You sound like _____ would give you the feeling of ____. Do I have that about right?

Exercise #11: Rehearse these questions with a trusted friend or family member. Be sure to practice follow-up questions like:
- Tell me more about _____. It sounds like you really want to experience _____. Is that about right?
- How does it feel knowing that you *really can* make _____ happen in your life?

2. Let's Explore Your Current Situation (Often, this includes pain and *"The Weeds"*)

The second part of the "The Cause of the Other Person" is related to her current situation.

In my conversation with my client, Abigail, I shared: **"The person wants to go to the Emerald City, but they're stuck in The Weeds.** The weeds are the painful parts of their current situation."

Between the Emerald City and the Weeds is a chasm. As an Executive Coach and Spoken Word Strategist, I have several processes to help my clients get past that chasm. I talk of "the bridge" and I talk about "the plane" — when I'm in a coaching session.

However, during the Free Strategy Session, **the person does NOT care about my process.** She focuses on two things: Living to the Emerald City and getting free of pain (The Weeds).

Here are some questions that help in the phase of hearing the person's Current Situation:
- How are things going for you now?
- What's not working?
- How does that feel?
- What hurts about that?
- Is there something causing you to be stuck?
- Do you feel that your slamming your head against a wall? Oww! So, you're not breaking through to the other side, right?

It's vital to take notes throughout your Free Strategy Session so you can go back to *the exact words* that the person expressed.

My own mentors invited me to use *the exact words* at times. Why? Because the person chose certain words *for a reason.*

Look at the difference between:
- So, it sounds like having your boss not listen to you bothers you. *[paraphrasing]*
  VERSUS
- So, it sounds like, when your boss *"tosses your good ideas out like used tissue paper"* — it really hurts. Do I have that

about right?

The phrase "tosses my good ideas out like used tissue paper" was the prospective client's *exact words.* You can feel the situation with these exact words.

Exercise #12: Rehearse the Current Situation questions with a trusted friend or family member. Be sure to practice follow-up questions like:
- It sounds like _____ really hurts. Is there something more to that?
- How long have you felt _____ about _____? Have you reached the point of "Enough is enough"?
- How badly do you want _____ to stop?

3. Let's Explore *How we might work together* to fulfill Your Vision

"So now, we're ready to talk about the third part of our agenda. As I mentioned: if and only if, we have a match, then we can talk about how we can work together. This is also the time when I share with you details related to the #1 obstacle between what's going on for you now and where you want to be. Also, I'll provide the exact steps for you to rise up to a higher level of success. Ready?" I said, to Nadia, a prospective client.

"I really want to work with you. I'm excited about how you want to do _____," I continued.

Be sure to develop your own ways of expressing your excitement about working with the client.

One of my mentors said, "You've got to claim your client." By this he meant that it was vital for me to express how I am the person's advocate and that I believe in what they're doing—and I want to be a part of the person's journey.

Exercise #13: Rehearse your own "let's work together" comments with a trusted friend or family member. Be sure to express your excitement about becoming the prospective client's big supporter. Remember enrolling, in part, is about you joining the clients' "cause."

* * * * * *

How the Enrolling Process fits into the Structure of a Video You Use for Marketing

Here again are the *Three Invitations:*
Let's explore ...
1) Your Vision ("The Vision for Your Best Life" ... *The Emerald City*)
2) Your Current Situation (Often, this includes pain and *"The Weeds"*)
3) How we might work together to fulfill Your Vision

Here are examples.

The Marketing Video can include script elements like:

a) "Would you like an abundance of clients?" *[Your Vision]*
b) "Are you needing more clients but somehow every week you don't complete your marketing?" *[Your Current Situation that includes pain and The Weeds]*
c) "Attend the workshop and you'll get excited about

implementing Authentic Marketing methods. Get more clients starting this week!" *[How we might work together to fulfill Your Vision]*

Tom Marcoux

Enrolling #6

The Enrolling Process and the Presenting Champagne Metaphor

Picture someone holding a champagne bottle. How that person holds the bottle gives you an impression:

- Holding the neck of the bottle and preparing to hit someone
- Holding the neck of the bottle in a casual way
- Holding the bottle with two hands, cradling it—the message is "This is a precious gift"

In Authentic Marketing, you start with yourself and your core values. The point is: what you offer feels like "a precious gift" so your marketing reflects that.

Here's something more: Consider the idea of someone cradling the bottle and carrying two glasses. This conveys that "you're in this together and you celebrate together."

In your email messages, design of your website and your videos, make sure you give a consistent message: "You're going to enjoy the results, and I'm right here with you. We'll celebrate the new and better things in your life—together."

Exercise #14: Write down your answers to:

How can you make what you offer appear as "the precious gift?" What can you change in your current marketing to demonstrate a higher level—the level of Authentic Marketing?

Enrolling #7

The Enrolling Process and the "What?-Questions"

My client, Alana, said, "I'm confused. I don't know what to do."

"I have two questions for you. First, what do you want?" I asked.

She told me.

Then I asked, "What is the right thing to do?"

Sometimes, the answers to the two above questions differ.

In Authentic Marketing, be sure to ask yourself the two questions.

Important Question:
Is it okay to help the person experience the whole situation including "the pain"?

The truth is: Many individuals do *not* go into action when they only talk about "a bright future."

One of my friends said, "I do NOT want to feel the pain of

regrets in the future. I make the changes I need to make so I don't feel I've wasted my life."

This comment relates to how many of us will pay the appropriate price (like investing in a coach to guide us)—so we will live up to our potential. (Several of us refer to a Higher Power-given potential).

To really go deep for your Authentic Marketing, you need to know yourself better. Here is a **special progression of "What?-Questions"**

In another section of this book, I shared a process that my client, Alexandra, went through.

I asked her, "What do you provide for your client?"

Then ... "What does your client from that?"

Then ... "What does your client get from that [second thing]?"

The point here is: We must go a few layers deeper to understand, feel and *know* what the deep, intrinsic value of something is.

I illustrate this as:

What do you get from that? Level 1
What do you get from that? Level 2
What do you get from that? Level 3
What do you get from that? Level 4
What do you get from that? Level 5

I guided my client Serena through the above progression:

Tom: What do you want?
Serena: To expand my income.

Tom: What do you get from that?

Serena: I can pay for my son, Mitch's, college education.

Tom: What do you get from that?

Serena: To feel relieved that he has the best start in life.

Tom: What do you get from that?

Serena: To feel like I'm a good mother.

Tom: What do you get from that?

Serena: To feel like I haven't screwed up my life.

Tom: What do you get from that?

Serena: To feel like I matter!

Exercise #15: Pull out your journal or a sheet of paper and take yourself through the 5 Levels of "What?-Questions." Then, see how you can tie in what's most important to you—and how you do your Authentic Marketing.

Tom Marcoux

Enrolling #8

Enrolling and *Extreme Confidence*

One powerful element of Enrolling is that you do *not* have to be perfect in your delivery to "smoothly persuade" someone to buy your product or service.

Instead, you develop Extreme Confidence because you practice ways to genuinely connect with the prospective client.

I guide clients and audiences in my concept of *Extreme Confidence* as "when you KNOW that you know how to adapt to anything."

To do well with Enrolling, you develop and rehearse *If-Then Patterns*.

You prepare what you will say before you enter certain situations when talking with a prospective client.

Here are examples:

If-Then Patterns
If the person says, "It's too expensive"

Then I say, "I agree. This is a significant decision. You mentioned that ____ is important to you ..."

If the person says, "I need to talk this over with my spouse ..."

Then I say, "And when you talk it over with your spouse what would you be talking about? .... How about we schedule a conference call so I can save you both time and answer any questions that come up?"

Exercise #16: Pull out your personal journal and answer these questions:

Where in the Enrolling process do I need more confidence?

What kind of If-Then Patterns would be good for me to prepare?

Then, write up four rough draft If-Then Patterns that apply to your specific situation with Authentic Marketing.

** For more about developing Extreme Confidence, see my book, *Amazing You.*

Enrolling #9

The Enrolling Process **via a Website**

Make your website "you" oriented. More than 14 years later, I still remember a link on the homepage of Oprah.com. The link read "Get Better Sleep." This is an example of the website focusing on "You, the visitor."

How is this an example of Enrolling? These three words "Get Better Sleep" tie into something that is important to millions of people, and it's something that is a cause of pain. Every week, I hear someone talk about their lack of sleep or sleep difficulties.

I keep a log of my own sleep. I do *not* oversleep so I want the sleep I get to count. Can you relate to that?

Enrolling starts with awareness of your prospective client's life situation.

A vital element of a successful website is for the homepage to be "sticky" (that is, the visitor stays glued to the webpage).

Research suggests that humans have an attention span of

6-8 seconds. Just in case you wondered, goldfish have an attention span of 9 seconds.

Some observations suggest that people decide to stay or leave a website within 2 to 7 seconds. I lean toward the idea of closer to 2 seconds.

If someone clicks an attractive link on your website, you got them. Now, they're immersed in your website.

So, think about Enrolling.

You start with the vision that the other person has for his or her own life. I previously mentioned that the person has a vision for their own Emerald City (comfort, fulfillment, joy, success and confidence).

Then, think about how you can write headlines that directly address the person's Compelling Needs.

I use the term Compelling Needs for a vital purpose. The noise of all forms of media require that you "punch through such noise."

For example, I'm personally interested in impacting more people while working less hours. If a website has a headline that addresses this goal, I'll pay attention That relates to my own Compelling Need.

Exercise #17: Answer this question:

How can you transform your wording on your website to directly address the website visitor as "you"?

Exercise #18: Answer these questions:

What does your website visitor really want?

Think of the person's Compelling Needs.

What is his or her fantasy?—for example, complete freedom from stress? (You could offer an audio download that provides 15 minutes of relaxation and freedom from stress, for example.)

I'm adding the idea of connecting with the person's fantasy because that can be compelling, too.

For example, at this moment, I recall a commercial that had a frazzled, grammar school teacher standing amid children running amuck.

Her mind (demonstrated by images in the commercial) was focused on a fantasy vacation.

She was on a tropical island, enjoying a luxurious backrub.

Sounds good!

How can you tie into your prospective clients' "fantasy"?

Tom Marcoux

Enrolling #10

The Enrolling Process via Email

It's reported that if one includes "video" in the subject heading of an email message, people are 19% more likely to open that particular email message.

How is this Enrolling? You're considering how people like to receive information. More people tend to watch videos. And many of us would rather *not* read more material.

As I write an email message, I think about the reader. What does she want to know next? How might she disagree? How might she want something elaborated on?

Here are Insights for Using Email.

- See if you can *thank the person* for something in your first sentence.

- If you need to say *no* to someone, see if you can call the person on the phone. (Saying *no* via email is what I call "The Double Slap" … you're saying *no* AND you're doing it through email.)

- Address the person by name. I realize that people are trying to spend less time with email. Be different. Be courteous. Refer to the person by their first name (if appropriate).
- Be careful about writing an email message when you're exhausted or angry. If something is troublesome, see if you can *read aloud* your rough draft of your email message to someone who wants **to protect you** from making a mistake.

Exercise #19: Write your answers to these questions:

How can you express yourself in a way to warm up your email communications? (Address the person by name, thank the person for something and so forth.)

How can you use the "Insights for Using Email" well?

Enrolling #11

The Enrolling Process **via an Enewsletter**

Are you receiving too many enewsletters'? Are they cluttering up your in-box?

Years ago, getting an enewsletter was like a gift from Heaven. Now, it can feel like a nuisance.

What changes an enewsletter from a mosquito to an invited guest? **Brief, relevant content.**

Let's face it: People often do *not* feel like reading anything more.

Offer a special video, and you stand out of the pack. I prefer to identify the length of the video. Keeping a video to 1:58 (less than 2 minutes) can get you more views.

We're all busy, and we want straight-to-the-point video material.

Put yourself into the shoes of your prospective client.

What do they want?

What annoys them?

How pressed are they from time-constraints and stress-filled facets of their day?

Be focused so that your email messages are a welcomed break from the person's packed schedule for the day.

The Vital Value of an Enewsletter

Researchers have suggested that **it takes 5 to 12 Impressions to Complete the Transaction.** That is, the person does *not* purchase a product or service based on glancing at one ad on Facebook (for example).

Your enewsletter can provide multiple impressions of what you offer.

Bonus:

Insights about Using Enewletters Well:

- Make your enewsletter brief.
- Remember that the enewsletter is to **Help** the person.
- Avoid trying to sell/promote something in each enewsletter.
- Keep on message. If you share a personal detail, make sure that in the same paragraph the reader understands how your comment is relevant to the subject of the enewsletter.
- Realize that it's natural for people to drop off your esubscribers list every time you send out an email message.
- Realize that for someone to purchase something, it often takes **5 to 12 impressions**. See if you can vary how you impact people. Use videos, links to your relevant blog articles or provide an audio program that one can listen to on one's smartphone.

Exercise #20: Make a list of those details (shared above) you can use to improve how you use your enewsletter.

Tom Marcoux

Enrolling #12

The Enrolling Process **via a Blog**

Keep on message. If you have multiple products in different categories have separate blogs.

For example, here are my blogs:

PitchPowerFest.com

GetTheBigYES.com

YourBodySoulandProsperity.com

You can get an idea how these blogs differ from each other simply from their domain names.

Think of your prospective clients' most pressing need. What major pain are they experiencing? What do they need to improve the most? How can you end the terrible struggle they are enduring?

None of us has time for everything. Our attention usually goes toward *our most pressing need*. Title your blog articles in ways that capture attention. Here are some examples:

- How You Can Do Your Best Work Even When You Feel Exhausted
- The Secret to Capturing Prospective Clients' Attention
- How to Free Yourself from Overworking AND Get More Done, Too!

Have a process to expand your reach. I have reviewed several books by top-tier authors on my blog YourBodySoulandProsperity.com. I even have a major publisher's marketing team members offer me a selection of their upcoming books for my potential reviews.

At this moment, YourBodySoulandProsperity.com reaches visitors from 98 countries. I realize that my reach expands because I'm associated with people who are expanding *their* reach. I carefully select which books I review so that my review will be *positive*. The authors tend to promote my review to their own esubscribers lists. This process works!

Exercise #21: Write down your answer to:

How will you prepare your blog articles to *keep on message* and address your clients' most pressing needs?

Enrolling #13

The Enrolling Process **on the Phone**

In a phone conversation, you can use many of the methods I shared about the in-person free strategy session earlier in this book.

Specifically related to your telephone conversation, implement these details:

- Be sure to make appropriate sounds like "mmm-hmmm" and phrases like "I hear you" and "That sounds frustrating" so the person knows you are completely concentrating on listening to him or her.
- Close your laptop. Turn off your smartphone chimes. Do NOT let anything distract you from your conversation.
- Take excellent notes and use the details that you learn during the conversation to let the person know you paid close attention.

Exercise #22: Think of previous phone conversations you've had. Write down *three things that bothered you* about how someone on the other end of the phone seemed to have their attention divided.

Identify *what you will do that resolves* the three annoying details.

Enrolling #14

The Enrolling Process and How the Elevator Dialogue and Supportive Listening Work
—so You Get the Most Value from Networking Events/Opportunities

First, we'll cover material related to how using an *Elevator Dialogue* is better than the old, standard "Elevator Speech" ...

At my blog YourBodySoulandProsperity.com, I shared this article:

Get Clients—Network Well—Do Better than an "Elevator Speech"

"I met this guy at a conference. Things were going fine until I asked, 'What do you do?' Then he launches into a commercial about himself. Total disconnect. I finally had to say, 'Excuse me. I just remembered: I have to make a phone call home," Amy, a friend, said. "Apparently, somebody had told this guy that he has to have a smooth 'Elevator Speech.' It wasn't smooth. It was fake."

In my speech titled "Power Up Your Brand: Attract Clients," I alert the audiences to how an Elevator Speech can break one's connection with a new contact. With an Elevator Speech, the idea is: You'd say these words as if you only had 30 seconds during an elevator ride to communicate the value of your work.

Here's the Big Problem: Most people are not trained performers so it sounds like a canned commercial! The listener feels bad. It's as if they think: "Hey! We were having a human conversation. Where did you go?! Now, I'm just listening to a robotic commercial."

Here's an example of a stilted Elevator Speech: "I am a financial wizard. I help you build a fortress around your assets." (Imagine that said in an over-the-top, artificial way.)

Instead, we'll use the Y.E.S. process:

Y – Yearn for "Elevator Dialogue"
E – Energize Listening
S – Sprinkle "diamonds"

1. Yearn for "Elevator Dialogue"

As an Executive Coach, I mention to clients: "When you meet someone in a networking event, be aware of whether the situation is "Talk At" or "Talk With."

Talk With refers to having an Elevator Dialogue. We "yearn for Elevator Dialogue" because we want what it gives us. It deepens the connection. You only talk about what feels relevant to the other person.

You avoid giving that person a stilted, canned Elevator Speech.

Instead, you make sure that you support a real and warm conversation. The person begins to trust you because you avoid "talking at" her, and you create a good business relationship from the start. Realize to "Power Up Your Brand," it's important to build it on trust. I've trained graduate students to develop a personal brand of T.H.O.R.: Trustworthy, Helpful, Organized, Respectful.

2. Energize Listening

There is a vital thing you need to do: Make sure what you say is relevant to the person you're talking with. How do you do that? You start listening as soon as possible.

Listening is a prime business relationship builder. Years ago, a telemarketer called me and said, "I know your business." Apparently, he had checked on my blog and other details. But he did *not* ask me questions. He did *not* listen. He failed to earn my trust. I thought, "If you won't listen to me, how can I trust you to help me?"

On the other hand, I share with audiences: *When you're listening, you're winning.*

Begin with "Gentle Questions." No one wants to be interrogated. Still, we seem to be "automatic question-answering beings."

A question is gentle when it's easy to answer and, perhaps, fun to answer.

You can ask: "Are you a business owner or do you work as part of a team?"

Business owners have truly different concerns from someone who works for a salary as part of a team.

Here are examples of other Gentle Questions:

- What are you looking forward to at this conference?
- Who is your ideal client?

You can gently start a conversation with a new contact at a networking event with something like: "Hello, I'm [your name] and you are?"

The person gets used to answering your gentle questions.

3. Sprinkle "diamonds"

Some novice business people make the error of reciting their resume.

Instead, I coach clients (and audience members) to pick a couple vital details to share naturally during a conversation.

Even when you're telling a story, keep it short. That's what I mean by "sprinkle"—like you would add a small amount of a condiment to a meal. Often, when giving an example, keep it to 20 seconds or less and turn the spotlight (of the conversation) back on the other person.

Here is an example:

George: "So, what do you do?"

Janet: "I'm wondering. Are you a business owner or do you work as part of a team?"

George: "I own my own business. It's web-based and I do [_____]. I'm still curious about what you do, Janet."

Janet: "I help business owners like you by designing graphics that make your home page 'stickier.' You know that people decide to leave a web page in 2 seconds or less. The graphics and designs I create get people to click and go deeper into your website. The conversation rate has often gone up 67%. More conversations to more sales. Are you working on bringing a new product to the market soon?"

In the above example, Janet sprinkled the "diamond" of

the improvement of 67% in the conversion rate. Then, you notice that she asks a question to return the "conversation spotlight" to focus on the other person.

In summary, business people do better when they use an Elevator Dialogue to make good and warm connections with new people.

* * * * *

How *Supportive Listening* Helps You Make Better Connections at Networking Events

When an audience member sees me on stage, using humor and stories to truly engage audience members, he or she often does not know this fact: I'm an introvert.

I say to audiences: "If you don't know if you're an introvert. If someone says, Party. And you say: How long is it? When can I leave? … You're an introvert!"

Introverts pay out energy when in a group. Introverts also recharge and recover their energy by enjoying some quiet time away from others.

My point is: I've learned to be careful of my personal energy *and* to truly connect with people. Instead of trying to impress people, I tell myself: I'm going to listen well to people. They'll be happy while they tell me their personal story."

I invite you to focus on good questions (and follow-up questions) to ask. In this way, you make the person feel good in your presence. They probably do not have too many good listeners in their circle.

Here are helpful questions (that inspire *Supportive Listening*):
- I'm [your name] and you are?

- How do you know our host, Mark?
- What are you looking forward to at this conference?
- How did you get started in your business?
- What's your favorite part of [what they're doing]?
- What's one of your hobbies?
- What are you looking forward to?

Exercise #23: Rehearse out loud, with a trusted friend or family member, the helpful questions that inspire Supportive Listening.

Special Note: Supportive Listening also includes what I call *Reflective Replies.* You reflect that *you heard* the person's implied feelings. Here are examples:
- That sounds frustrating. Then what happened?
- That sounds intense. What did you want to happen next?

People want you to *know* their feelings not merely the surface content of their message. On some level, many of us want to engage with someone who can empathize with our experiences. The effective Enroller *listens* with his or her whole being: heart, mind, and soul.

* For more about networking well, see my book *Relax Your Way Networking.*

Enrolling #15

The Enrolling Process as Tied into Speaking to a Group, Getting Applications for a Free Strategy Session and Beyond

"I hate cold calling," my client, Alexandra, said.

"I hear you. How about I share with you something that can free you of that process," I said.

"Tell me!" she said, smiling.

Then I shared with her the process of **Speak to a Group → Gather Applications for a Free Strategy Session ... and call people who WELCOME your phone call!**

When my mentors taught me this process, I breathed out a big sigh of relief. Can you relate to that?

Why does this process work well? Because it ties directly into Authentic Marketing and Enrolling ... *Don't sell—help.*

When you give a speech, you accomplish two things: You establish your *Credibility as an Expert* and you help people.

Then they want more guidance from you.

Near the end of your speech, you say, "I now want to give you your next step. Your best step that I recommend. My team member, Anna, is sharing with you the application so you can have a free strategy session with me."

Often, I add, "The first 15 people who turn in your filled-out application—you'll get access to the first module of my well-received online course *Get the Big YES*. The subtitle is *Use Extreme Confidence to Get Clients and Get Things Done!*"

One of my clients said, "When I give a speech, they trust me."

Exactly! That's why this business model of speak to groups→ gather applications for a Free Strategy Session → and call people who WELCOME your phone call works well.

A Vital Part of Having Audience Members Apply for a Limited Number of Free Strategy Sessions

Trudy, one of my clients said, "But I don't have time to do 15 one-hour strategy sessions."

"That's why you use an application. If someone does not qualify, you thank them for applying—and you send them a free eBook," I replied.

Here's a process I call *Reduce the Size of the Haystack.* The old phrase is "finding a needle in the haystack." How do you find a needle in a haystack? I've liked the idea "use a powerful magnet."

However, in finding one's ideal client, one does need to limit how many people you give a free strategy session to.

Here's an example: 70 people in the room. 17 apply. 12 people identified their commitment to improving their business at the high level of 10 (on a scale of 1 to 10).

Immediately you can eliminate 5 people from strategy sessions because they picked a lower commitment level.

Then pick the Top 6 based on their answers to the application questions.

Exercise #24: Identify questions that you would put into an application for a free strategy session with you.

Consider questions that would reveal a low level of commitment.

If you want to filter out people who have never paid for advice and coaching, you could even put in a question like: "Have you ever hired a consultant or coach before?"

Tom Marcoux

Enrolling #16

The Enrolling Process and the Power of Using Videos on YouTube — and More

"I think I should use videos," my client, Alexandra, said. "But ... I'm too self-conscious. I feel awkward talking directly to the camera."

"I hear you. It was awkward for me, too—at the beginning. In fact, I had to set up momentum so I'd just get the video done, and I'd avoid letting fear or perfectionism slow me down. Is fear or perfectionism causing you some trouble?" I replied.

This began an in-depth conversation and process to help Alexandra move forward.

First, let's begin with the value of using video marketing. If something is important enough to you, you'll push yourself forward through first efforts and learning to improve over time.

The Power of Video Marketing

While viewing an article at Forbes.com, these details caught my attention:

- Placing "video" in an email subject line can boost open rates by 19%.
- "Small Business Trends" identified: 1) 51.9% of marketers (worldwide) note that video has the best ROI and 2) viewers (before a purchase) are 1.81 more likely to make a purchase—than non-video-viewers.

It's powerful to note that people viewing a video are nearly two times more likely to buy something.

Two Special Advantages of Video

First, *you can demonstrate your point.* This is more powerful that a standard story. In another section of this book, I talk about "using the Power of Discovery."

I mention that in my video related to Authentic Marketing, I make a promise: "Before the end of this video, I'll share the Essence of Enrolling." When I speak on that topic, the viewer has the chance to *discover* something he or she did not know before.

Second, *in a video you can "anticipate the viewer's concern." Then you can provide assurance and support.*

Here are examples:

- "You might feel that you don't have time to take an online course at this moment. I hear you. That's why I designed this course as videos and audios you experience through your smartphone. You can do this at any time when you're waiting—before a meeting, for example."

- "You might feel getting over being camera-shy is too tough. Through this workshop, you'll have the opportunity to practice ..."

When you address the viewer's concern, you remove any chance that the concern might "fester" and "kill the sale."

How to Deal with Discomfort about Looking Directly at the Video Camera

As a trained actor, performer and feature film director, I guide people to their best performances.

The process of getting used to being on camera can *start with NOT looking at the camera.*

In interviews that you see on broadcast news, you'll note that people look to the side of the camera. They're talking with the reporter (or interviewer). The camera is merely an observer (like another person might observe a conversation at the dinner table). This is where you can start.

As you get used to being on camera, you can start practicing and directly address the camera. It helps to imagine your best friend as viewing you through the camera lens.

How to Press Through Stages of Performance

I've observed that some video performers need a certain number of "takes" (repetitions of the performance before the camera).

My client, Theo, needs three: a) not clear of his words, b) inappropriately "pushing" his words and c) relaxing into "friendly energy."

While I was directing a feature film (that went to the Cannes film market ultimately), I noted that two of my actors were best on the first take. A third actor was best on her eighth take. What did I do?

I filmed the two "First Take" guys as a two-shot first. (Both actors in the shot.)

I saved the closeups for the third actor for last. Basically, she had to warm up.

So, when you do your videos, see if you must warm up.

Also know that you have choices in editing. Many videos now on YouTube have a fast pace and "hard cuts." That means any boring sections or mistakes are simply cut out.

You could also use a "quick dissolve" between shots—if that feels appropriate to you.

In my workshop*, *Authentic Marketing*, I include this exercise:

(* In the workshop, I have people gather in "Teams of Three." They get two partners and they rotate through the roles—during the workshop.)

Exercise #25: Practice "answer the viewer's concern." Secondly, practice promising something and then delivering on it. Here's the example: "Before the end of this video, I will share with you the Essence of Enrolling." Then record the special information that fulfills the promise.

Note: If you're not comfortable in addressing the camera, at first, look just to the side of the camera. Have a friend or colleague placed there, and talk with that person (while the camera records your performance).

Enrolling #17

Enrolling and "Don't Sell—Help"

Cynthia, my client, continued getting ready to present her $10,000 coaching program to the next people she had pre-scheduled for Free Strategy sessions.

Over the course of the recent coaching sessions, I listened carefully to Cynthia.

Then a shining moment occurred.

"I'm looking forward to helping the person feel really supported," Cynthia said.

"That's it, Cynthia. You give the person such support in the free strategy session that they naturally want more of that," I replied smiling.

The above conversation is an example of the power and even joy associated with Enrolling and Authentic Marketing.

Cynthia does *not* have to push or try to convince the other person.

Cynthia starts from the approach of helping the person.

It comes down to: "Don't sell—help."

Exercise #26: Write down your answers to:

How can you help someone during your free strategy session?

If you're doing a video, how can you alert the prospective client to an important situation he or she needs to take care of? You'll be helping the person by assisting them to understand the scope of what a solution requires.

Enrolling #18

Enrolling and "It's Too Expensive"

"I dread it," Cynthia, my client, said.

"What?"

"When someone says, 'It's too expensive."

"Is that true? Are your coaching services too expensive?" I asked.

"No!" Cynthia said with strength.

"You're right about that," I said.

"With all the extra effort and bonuses I provide, the client is getting a bargain," Cynthia said.

"That's true," I said with equal strength. "So, what's going on here?"

"I guess that the person does not *feel* the value yet," she said.

"That's an important part of it. Something is *not* too expensive when we *know* that we're getting more value than the fee that we're paying," I said.

The Enrolling Method vs. Overcoming the Objection

Some traditional salespeople talked about "overcoming the objection" as if they were in an epic battle with the prospective client.

Instead, the Enrolling Method has a whole different perspective.

Here are some Enrolling-style comments:

The person says: "It's too expensive."

Enroller replies: "I agree that this is a significant decision. And you mentioned that what you really want is to _____. "

- "You've already mentioned that staying stuck in the rut is costing you $100,000 a year. As we talked about, the ladder out of the rut is you're becoming more valuable with new skills ..."
- "Would you enroll in this online class if money wasn't holding you back?"

After you have guided the prospective client so *she expresses the full value* of what you're offering, you can use comments like these to work with her money concerns:

- "Since I'm a coach. Let's look at how you can bring this [offering] in your life. Let's have a bit of a coaching session now. Sound good?"
- "I've just sent you an email. My own coach shared with me three options (I have them for you in the email) for having the funds to invest in yourself and your business now."
- "So, one of my best clients felt deep in his heart that

he really needed this coaching to rise up and take his business to where it needs to be. He used PayPal—at the moment one can get credit for [amount] for six months with no payments and no interest. He also used a credit card for the rest of the fee. How does this sound to you?"

Exercise #27: Identify six ways that you can respond to the "it's too expensive" comment from a prospective client. Try variations of the language you find above in this section of the book. Say the words out loud to a trusted friend in a rehearsal session. See how you can modify the words so they work well, specifically for you.

Enrolling #19

Enrolling and "I need to wait"

"She said, 'I need to wait.' Then, she went into some reasons, and they sound reasonable to me," my client, Harry, said.

"So, you were buying into her reasons?" I asked.

"Was that wrong?"

"It depends," I said. "Some people just find it hard to make a decision. They wait for someone to magically make it okay or somehow comfortable for them to make the decision. When they make a decision, they get a rush of *relief*. Some people are looking for 'permission' to invest money into themselves. You might need to be the person who supports them to make a decision for their ultimate good."

Furthermore, there are people who just need you to "hold a sacred space." They'll ask, "Do you really feel this will work for me?

"Yes," is a great reply, and you need to do your

homework so you can say that clearly, with full integrity. For Authentic Marketing to work, you need to do what's necessary. Your service must be founded our your training and how you achieve valuable results for clients.

Additionally, you can ask, "In order for you to know that this is right for you and to move forward now, what has to happen?"

Another thing you can ask is: "If you were waiting, what would you be thinking about?"

Some Enrollers ask, "What does waiting *cost* you?"

Remember They Came to You Because You're the Expert

Life is uncertain. Some people look to their peers for approval or support.

Entrepreneurs must learn to trust their gut and their heart.

You might need to be that support that the person needs to move forward.

Be sure to "own it" that you are the expert. If the person didn't need you or didn't find you to be a credible expert, you would not be in the free strategy session at this moment.

Practice saying something like: "Here is your next step. Your best step, that I recommend."

Yes—that's you making a recommendation. Why? Because you have worked hard to be the expert that will help this person rise up to his or her Emerald City (comfort, success, fulfillment and confidence).

If Their Reason for Waiting Really Is Legitimate ...

Be sure to set up a follow-up appointment. Make sure that

the person has homework. You can say something like: "So I'm glad to hear, Jacinta, that you'll be double-checking the _____. So, we'll both be prepared when we talk on Wednesday at 3 pm. Yes? Great. I'll call you then."

Exercise #28: Write down your answer to:

What can you do so you feel certain in your heart that you are the expert and the person does well to follow your recommendation?

Tom Marcoux

Enrolling #20

Enrolling and "I need to talk to someone"

"What do I do if they say, 'I need to talk to someone'?" Kenneth, my client, asked.

"See if you can find out if this person is part of the decision. You could ask something like, 'Oh. So, you and Sarah usually make decisions like this together?'" I replied.

In an extended discussion, I shared that talking with another person could be a ruse or a way that the person gets out of the "hot seat" of making a decision. Or it could be a natural and appropriate part of the process.

Consider using questions like these:

- And when you talk it over with your spouse, what would you be talking about?
- How about we schedule a conference call so I can save you both time and answer any questions that come up?"

It's important that you rehearse several questions and

responses ahead of time.

If you sound certain, you can help the person feel stronger.

An Important Truth About the Prospective Client Talking with Someone Else

The person is *not* going to be able to express the full value of what you do as well as you can. Also, you'd like to be present for the conversation so you can answer questions and concerns directly.

Exercise #29: Rehearse with a trusted friend four different responses to the person's comment: "I have to talk to someone."

Enrolling #21

Enrolling and a Viewpoint: Fill the Pipeline vs. "Succession of Audiences"

"Oh, no! I just lost a client!" Anita, my client, said. After an extended conversation in which Anita clarified that she *thought* she was *going to be hired* by the person, I shared an insight:

If you have one and you lose one, it's a tragedy.
If you have twenty and you lose one, it's just a step.

The idea is to be *constantly extending your reach* to more potential clients.

Some people use the phrase "fill the pipeline" which is based on the metaphor that one needs to fill an Alaskan pipeline constantly because it takes a long time for the oil to get from Alaska to the middle of the continental United States of America.

On the other hand, in Enrolling, we continually keep our understanding that we're working with people. Not oil. Not opponents.

I prefer to say, "You constantly develop a *Succession of Audiences.*"

How does this look?

I give a workshop "Pitch with Extreme Confidence" to a group of Stanford Entrepreneurs. The audience members enter my *Pyramid of Success* at Level 1.

Deep, Deep Transformation 1-year clients (Level 5)

****

Those people who become a 6-months client (Level 4)

****

Those people who experience a Free Strategy Session (Level 3)

****

Audience members who apply for a Free Strategy Session (Level 2)

****

Tom's workshop "Pitch with Extreme Confidence" (Level 1)

As you can see, we have five levels. At each level, the audience becomes smaller. Their investment of time and fees rise. More importantly, *their transformation and improvement of their own results rise.*

You can have multiple venues for your Level 1:
- YouTube video
- Webinar
- Be a guest on a popular podcast

- Be a guest on a TV or Radio show

I invite you to consider dropping the "Fill the pipeline" metaphor. Instead, focus on making a warm connection with a Succession of Audiences.

A Special Note: TEDx as a facet of your Authentic Marketing

I've worked with a number of people preparing a TEDx Talk.

One of my mentors brought this to my attention:

- On average, the video of your TEDx Talk has the potential of 10,000 to 100,000 views (over a four-year period)
- You'll be networking with 33 speakers (It depends on the venue.)
- You'll be networking with master networkers, that is, the conference organizers.

There is the possibility that your TEDx Talk might help you rise to the level of the actual 5-day TED mainstage event.

Exercise #30: Write your answers to these questions:

What can be your Succession of Audiences?

How can you make it possible for more people to enter your Pyramid of Success at Level 1?

What can you focus on as your *multiple venues* for your Level 1 audiences?

Enrolling #22

Structuring a Webinar to Invite People to Enroll in Your Six-Week Online Course

"I'm baffled," my client, Arthur, said.

"How so?"

"I get it. I need a free webinar to enroll people into my six-week online course. Where do I start?"

This began an extended conversation.

To give you highlights about putting together a webinar, look at this outline:

11 Elements of an Effective Webinar
1) Use a "grabber" (to get attention)
2) Create rapport with the viewer (perhaps, with a brief personal story to show that you experienced what the viewer is now feeling)
3) Demonstrate Your Credibility
4) Identify Problems
5) Offer "the Partial Solutions" [Provide some "insights."

You will *not* be solving the problems because the solution requires that the viewer has *the experiences* only found in your 6-week Online Course.)

6) Provide Video Testimonials (this is often call "social proof")

7) Present an Irresistible Offer

8) Provide a No-Risk Guarantee

9) Express the Special Bonuses when One Buys now

10) Give the Deadline

11) Provide the "Big Finish"—make the Big Benefits Clear and Emphasize the Bonuses. Provide a Call to Action.

Exercise #31: If you're interested in enrolling people in an online course, begin the process. Jot down your first ideas related to the above *List of 11 Elements of an Effective Webinar.*

Enrolling #23

Enrolling and *Soft-Hearted Persuasion vs. Hard-Headed Convincing*

One week ago, I addressed an audience and pointed out that according to some research—on average—women used to live ten years longer than men. But, recently, women are only living *six years* longer.

I turned to a friendly circle of women in the audience and said, "What are you doing?!"

They laughed.

When people are laughing, it's easier for them to take in new material. You can *avoid* trying to push an idea or your product.

A couple of years ago, I did a video about the difference between *Hard-Headed Convincing* and *Soft-Hearted Persuasion.*

Enrolling is based on Soft-Hearted Persuasion.

Soft-Hearted Persuasion is built on listening first so you understand and feel what is most important to the person.

On the other hand, Hard-Headed Convincing is arrogant

in that the person attempts to "hammer home" the logic of what he or she is pushing. Let's *stay away* from that!

A Special Part of Soft-Hearted Persuasion

This next process is based on some material that researchers discovered. People tend to resist. Here's how you can go around such resistance.

Let's say a friend says, "I'm thinking about losing weight."

You could ask, "On a scale of 1 to 10—10 means you are totally ready—how ready are you to do what it takes to drop weight?"

"4," your friend responds.

"Why is it not a 2?" you ask.

"What?"

"Why are you at the level 2?"

"Well, my doctor said that I'm risking my health. If I stay on this path, I could get diabetes. I could get a heart attack. I might miss seeing my daughter grow up," your friend says.

This is a powerful version of Soft-Hearted Persuasion: *The person persuades herself.*

Exercise #32: Write down your answers to:

Have you noticed that you have been pushing as you try to get a client?

Are you ready to apply the idea of listening more (and first!) as part of your doing Soft-Hearted Persuasion?

You could have a rehearsal with a trusted friend and have them call it out: "Hey, you're pushing."

Then you ask questions (as noted in other sections of this book).

Enrolling #24

Enrolling and the *Subconscious Web of Opportunities*

"What do you think I should do, Tom?" my client, Anita, said.

"Based on what you've expressed so far as to what's most important to you, it looks like getting your speaker demonstration video done is crucial, at this time. And, I want to introduce this idea: The Subconscious Web of Opportunities."

How You Can Take Advantage of the Subconscious Web of Opportunities

In working with clients and with my own mentors and coaches over the years, I've observed a powerful process.

You can notice the times when you blurt out the truth.

I remember the first time I said to my coach, "I love what I do as a novelist!" I realized that was the first time I *owned* that part of my journey. I was writing a novel. I had the courage to make the transition from screenplay writing to writing a novel.

I owned the new role of "novelist."

Of vital importance, my subconscious mind *owned* the fact that I am a novelist.

Researchers note that 93% of our decisions take place on the subconscious level. You want your subconscious mind to function *as your friend!*

As you develop your materials so you make the shift away from selling to Enrolling, make space for your intuition and your subconscious mind.

Here's an important detail: Enrolling is about asking valuable questions.

You ask questions that guide a prospective client to *express* her Emerald City (where she wants to live in comfort, success, fulfillment and confidence).

You also ask questions so the person expresses The Weeds (the pain and frustration of her Current Situation).

Often, during these conversations, I hear people say, "Oh, I never said that quite that way before."

Great! People are expressing details from their subconscious mind.

This material rising from the subconscious mind can help both of us move forward into the client's bright future.

When I talk about "the Subconscious Web of Opportunities," I'm mean that neither the coach nor the client will always find the best solution through logic alone.

Use all your resources including the deep feelings and observations rising from the subconscious mind.

Risk expert Gerd Gigerenzer has noted that gut feelings often arise from data that has not risen to the conscious mind level.

We can take advantage of this Gigerenzer's observation

by making space to consider what our intuition offers up.

You'll become a better Enroller when you do this. And you'll serve your clients in more effective ways.

Exercise #33: Write down your answers to:

What will you do to make space for your intuition? Will you make sure to pause for a nap or a night's sleep to see what good ideas arise later?

Will you have conversations with people and note what intuitive insights *arise out of your own feeli*ngs in the conversation?

Action Strategies #1

Develop the Action Strategies to Get Your Messages to the Prospective Clients to Grow Your Business

"What's the best form of marketing, Tom?" Anita, my client asked.

I replied,

**"The best marketing for you is
the marketing you DO."**

In truth, theories don't count.
Action counts.

You might find this section of this book to be the most helpful for you now.

First, procrastination arises from pain or the anticipation of pain.

The whole idea of Enrolling is about getting the pain of old, standard selling OUT of your life. This will eliminate

a lot of standard procrastination.

You don't have to become another person to sell anything. You keep connected with your core values. You live by this understanding:

Selling is imposition.
Enrolling is invitation.

You'll do the Authentic Marketing efforts related to Enrolling.

Second, here is a vital insight:

Systems overpower willpower.

Willpower is unreliable. According research at Stanford University, willpower wears out as the day goes along. That's why I eat salad for breakfast.

Eating salad for breakfast is *one of my systems*. It takes no conscious thought. Each morning I have tomatoes and spinach. No waffling. No wasted time. And no chance that I'll fail to have vegetables in my daily meals.

This brings us to …

Use a System to Focus on "Your Powerful Three"

I first introduced the "Power of Three" in the below blog article:

Use the "Power of Three" for Real Success!

"How do I know which product is going to really work in the marketplace?" my new client, Andy, asked.

"You don't," I replied. "What really helps is to use 'The Power of Three.'"

The Power of Three is a process that empowers you to try things in the marketplace, to stay strong and to maintain your focus.

We'll use the T.O.P. process:
T – take three to the marketplace
O – optimize three and no more
P – power-up "imperfect action"

1. Take three to the marketplace

When you take three products to the marketplace, you have three times the chance that you'll find something that truly resonates with your target market.

People like a choice.

As a professional speaker, I provide the event planner/meeting planner with my three top speech topics:

- Get the Big YES: Use Extreme Confidence to Get Clients and Get It Done!
- Get It Done, Get Stronger, Get Credit for It—Power Time Management
- Pitch with Extreme Confidence: The Pitch Hacking Method

Which one will resonate more with the meeting planner or her group? I don't know … until I have a *conversation* with the meeting planner. Often, while we're having a phone call, I send one or more of my speaker one sheets (they look like flyers).

Let the marketplace let you know what can turn "red hot."

2. Optimize three and no more

Focus is a crucial part of business success. It's important to avoid getting distracted. Similarly, you'll do better to avoid diluting your power, resources and attention. Pick three things and avoid trying to push too many things at once. Over the years, I've written 44 books. Still, I focus on marketing only three top speeches at this time.

Now it's your turn. What are the three best candidates (products/services) that you can promote now?

3. Power-up "imperfect action"

Waiting for the perfect time or the perfect form of your product can cause you to falter. Sometimes, perfectionists fail because they're not shipping out their product.

Years ago, one of my friends said, "Creating a cure for no known disease." He was referring to those engineers who fall in love with an idea, create a company, but later find out that no market wants what they're offering.

The solution is to take something to the marketplace and get feedback.

"Real artists ship." – Steve Jobs

Jobs was referring to the idea that real artist deliver value. They send products into the marketplace. They learn from real users of the product. They improve the product for the next iteration.

To know if you have something people want, see if you can get real customers to let you know what they prefer.

For example, I wanted to give a speech on "pitch hacks." A meeting planner was concerned that the title that I had was not clear enough. I worked with my team and the title became "Pitch with Extreme Confidence: The Pitch Hacking Method."

One of my mentors mentioned taking "imperfect action." We do *not* wait for the perfect form of some item. For example, I have worked with clients who did not think their biography was "perfect enough yet."

I asked, "Does your biography communicate what you bring to the table? Is it clear about your credentials and what you can do for the client?"

When the client says "yes," then the biography is "good enough," and the client can use his or her speaker one sheet as a tool for getting speaking engagements. Sure, the client can later revise her biography. Still, she has *not* let the biography become a roadblock, stopping her from moving forward.

In summary, use the Power of Three so you enter the marketplace, create momentum and refine as you go along.

Take action and move forward.

Exercise #34: Let's continue the wisdom of using the Power of Three.

Write down three possible marketing messages you could promote.

Write down three possible places where you could reach out for "an audience."

Here are possibilities:
- LinkedIn
- Facebook
- giving in-person speeches
- posting videos on YouTube (that you promote in

enewsletter, your website, Twitter, LinkedIn, Facebook and so forth)

Action Strategies #2

Use Goals Better Than Before: The Power of "3 Levels of Goals" ... and How this Ties in with Authentic Marketing

"Why do you want to do Authentic Marketing?" I asked, Mariam, an audience member.

"Because I just want do what I'm trained for. I want to support my clients. I don't want to become Ms. Fast-talking Saleswoman," Mariam said.

"I'm right there with you," I said.

Then I shared with Mariam and the audience a process that helps us shake off the dust created by old, traditional goal-setting.

Traditional goal-setting would have us make 20 marketing call 5 days a week.

Is that going to happen?

Many of us will simply "get too busy," and then we drain

own energy with our self-recriminations.

Instead, I'll introduce you to The 3 Levels of Goals …

Use the 3 Levels of Goals: Good, Excellent and Amazing!

A few months ago, my book *Amazing You* came out. In it I introduced the following insights:

"I just don't get around to making my marketing phone calls. … I … I think I'm afraid that I'll mess them up," my client Anita, said.

"Let's work on this together," I said. "To release you from hesitation caused by fear, we're going to talk about *Setting Goals on 3 Levels: Good, Excellent and Amazing!* So, in one day, what would be an *Amazing!* number of marketing phone calls for you to make?"

"Eighteen."

"So that's *Amazing!* What would be a 'good' number of calls?"

"Six."

"Are you sure you could make six calls during the day?"

"I'm not sure."

"How about two phone calls?" I asked.

"Two? Sure, I could do that," Anita said.

"Good to hear. So, 'two phone calls' is at your 'Good' level," I said.

"I'm not sure that two is *Good*," Anita said.

"Two is **better than zero**," I said.

Anita smiled. "Yeah. You're right."

"Here's the helpful detail. Anything over 2 phone calls is on the 'Excellent' Level." This is how you can have Excellent Days."

* * *

Here's a special note: When you set the action to achieve "Good" at a modest level, you avoid disappointing yourself! That's important. Why? Many of us naturally tend to avoid what hurts. **Self-Disappointment hurts a lot.** Many of us are, subconsciously, making lots of efforts to avoid such pain.

Let's face it. Many of us hold great fear about disappointment. So, we live a lesser life. No more of that!

Use this *process of Good-Excellent-Amazing!* to get out of a rut.

Working with clients, I note that each client can become stronger to handle what I call the External Factor Disappointment. Sure, it hurts when a prospective client says a final and firm 'No.' One solution is to get in front of additional, high quality, prospective clients. I said to a team member:

"If you hear 'No' from one and you only have one — it's a tragedy.

If you hear 'No' and you have twenty to go, 'No' is just a step."

In summary:

Set your goals on the Good – Excellent – Amazing! Levels

Acknowledge when subconscious fear may be slowing you down.

Become skilled at taking action and remember: "Better than Zero!"

Realize that setting goals on the Amazing! Level is a process to expand your thinking.

The process of Good, Excellent and Amazing! is a system. It works for my clients. I use it.

Some days, I tell myself: One more phone call, that will be

Good!

I like the days when I cross into *Excellent!*

In the recent three days, my editor and I completed 9 videos for my online class *"Get the Big YES: Use Extreme Confidence to Get Clients and Get It Done!"*

With my team member's help, I crossed over to Amazing!

Amazing! happens more often when you **write down your Amazing! Goals.**

How Using 3 Levels of Goals Ties in with Authentic Marketing

Here's an unusual insight: *When you take better care of yourself, you take better care of your prospective clients.*

This ties in with Enrolling.

If you're pushing yourself to do old, traditional sales— you are likely to push people you talk with.

Avoid that!

First, connect with your core values. At the beginning of this section, I mentioned how my audience member, Mariam, said, "I just want do what I'm trained for. I want to support my clients."

Ultimately, I showed Mariam how she can carry over her listening skills into how she enrolls new clients.

"What a relief!" Mariam said.

I further encourage Mariam to set 3 Levels of Goals so that she has the experience of "doing well" each day.

Exercise #35: Write down your first ideas of what can be your 3 Levels of Goals: Good, Excellent and Amazing!

Action Strategies #3

Connect with Your *End Game* and Using a *Step Tree*

"What is your End Game—what do you really want? That is, when it's all working ideally—what are you doing? What are you enjoying?" I asked my client, Mark.

At a certain point in the coaching session, Mark said, "I don't know how to get there. But I want ... what I really want is to be a High-Profile Speaker-Author, speaking at conferences around the world."

"Good! That's where we'll start. We're going to use one or more Step Trees."

"What's that?"

"It's something I've developed. We use a Step Tree because the journey manifests organically—often *not* in a simple linear progression," I said.

Use a *Step Tree* to Move Forward Fast

We begin with your "End Game—what you really want

on the Ideal Level."

You start with the target. Then the steps start to form leading up to the target.

Here's the good news: When you see the target and you see the steps, feelings of overwhelm and racing thoughts can quiet down.

You have probably heard of a "mindmap." This is a process of writing down ideas in circles and then you use lines to connect ideas.

With my clients, I use my process called a *Step Tree*.

Success often is *not* a direct and linear process.

Here is s **Partial Example of a STEP TREE:**

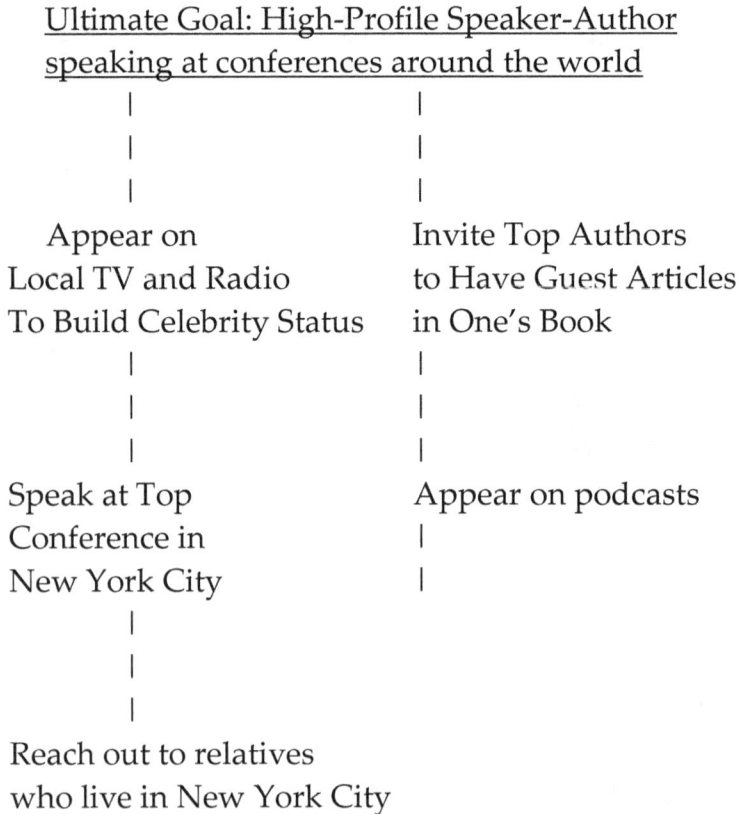

<u>Ultimate Goal: High-Profile Speaker-Author</u>
<u>speaking at conferences around the world</u>

| |

| |

| |

Appear on   Invite Top Authors
Local TV and Radio   to Have Guest Articles
To Build Celebrity Status in One's Book

| |

| |

| |

Speak at Top   Appear on podcasts
Conference in |
New York City |

|

|

|

Reach out to relatives
who live in New York City

Exercise #36: Write up two *Step Trees:*

Start with an Ultimate Goal #1: The person purchases your product or service.

Some possible steps:

- Come up with the title of a workshop
- Write up the outline for the workshop
- Think of the image that goes out in your marketing messages
- Develop a 1 to 3-minute video that presents
  A) The Question that Touches Their Pain
  B) The Big Benefits for Attending the Workshop

Ultimate Goal #2: Automate How I Get People into my Pyramid of Success (see a previous section).

At Level 1: Will I use Facebook ads *(Be careful with this!)?*

Will I speak at the local Chamber of Commerce?

Will I develop a video that teaches something that is compelling—which will get people to click to my website?

Tom Marcoux

Pulling it All Together #1

The Conclusion – Pulling It All Together

"What causes procrastination?" I asked the audience.

"I don't feel like doing it," a woman said.

"It's going to be painful," a man said.

"Good points. I have something add to that. Pain causes procrastination. Also, we anticipate pain of doing some tasks. Fear is involved."

Are you ready to get fear and procrastination out of your way?

I shared the follow material at my blog
YourBodySoulandProsperity.com

Drop Fear and Procrastination—for Real Success!

"I just can't get myself to get to the gym," Sam says.

"I don't know what happens. Somehow, I just don't get

around to rehearsing before giving the presentation. And then I have to wing it," Anita says.

Why do we procrastinate? Researchers note much of it arises from 1) anticipation of pain and 2) not knowing what to do. Even not knowing what to do causes pain. So, we're back to pain causing procrastination.

Additionally, what does fear do to us? Many of us report that we're afraid of something going wrong and causing us pain.

I submit to you that procrastination arises from fear.

Conventional Approach: Try to tough out fear and pain.
vs.
Extreme Confidence Approach: Place a system so you automatically do something positive when a Trigger hits you.

A system can be as simple as "send a follow-up email immediately upon hanging up the phone." A system does not have to be elaborate. The point is to make your next action into something that's automatic.

Successful people I've interviewed have demonstrated that they are skilled at dealing with fear and procrastination. They move forward at an extraordinary pace. Successful people do *not* rely on "I feel like it."

Additionally, relying on willpower is the path to disaster. Why? Willpower wears out as the day goes along. Researchers note that we experience a form of fatigue arising from the exercise of our will with choice after choice.

Fortunately, I've developed a process that helps my clients and audiences. I call it S.P.A. (Many of us would like to relax at a spa. Creating success through S.P.A. leads to more "spa moments.")

S – start well
P – preset
A – act

1. Start well

My client, Marina, said, "It's just getting started that's hard for me."

I replied, "What you need is a system. That is, we set a pattern."

She mentioned that she was having trouble "getting around to renewing her driver's license."

"How about use this as your system?" I began. "Put the page from the Dept. of Motor Vehicles right in front of your desktop monitor. Place your passwords-book next to the DMV form. So tomorrow, it's like you have already started. Remember two ideas: 1) *Worst First*—do the tough task first and 2) Make it easy for you to get in motion. (I call this the "Easy Part Start.")

An important element of "start well" is to set a "starting ritual." Researchers note that many successful people have some daily habit that gets them into action fast.

One of my clients, Amanda tells herself, "Just write. Toss clay on the table." This is Amanda's way of assuring herself that she can return and revise her writing (like a sculptor shaping the clay into a work of art).

2. Preset

To overcome procrastination, use this method: **"Preset the Trigger Sequence."**

First, I'll identify a Trigger Sequence. Something in your environment (or even a recurring thought) pushes you into a reaction. The trigger plus your reaction is the Trigger Sequence.

Fortunately, you can take control. Before you get into a "hot situation," make decisions about what your positive action could be. Such a positive action would replace an automatic negative reaction.

For example, my friend, Helena, returns home and feels like reaching for cookies. Fortunately, she has "preset" the situation with apples set out on the dining room table. Instead of reaching for a cookie, she grabs an apple. It works for her.

The point is: She knows she will be hit by the Trigger of "I'm home, and I'm hungry." However, she has already "Preset the Trigger Sequence" to help her take a healthy action.

Act

Sam, one of my clients, said, "I'm afraid of just acting in a haphazard way. Doing something wrong is worse than doing nothing!"

Within an extended conversation, I guided Sam with two principles:

- Motion Brings Clarity
- If in doubt, leave it out.

Motion Brings Clarity

As an Executive Coach and Spoken Word Strategist. I help people get unstuck. I say, "I'm in the business of transformation; I'm *not* in the business of Band-aids."

Recently, I was working with a client who had a Big Success! Unfortunately, the client fell into a valley of indecision and procrastination. Now, she was stuck, and she said, "I'm not sure if I'm on the right path."

We talked for a significant time. Then I shared with her an

important distinction. I drew two lines to form a vertical road on the left portion of a sheet of paper. Then I drew a matching vertical road on the right side of the page.

I said, "On the left you want a road that has the words 'certainty' and 'clarity'. The road on the right side includes 'Motion' and 'Discovery.'"

Here's an important distinction: *Motion Brings Clarity.* You take some small action. You move up the mountain, and then you can see 3 New Peaks (choices).

I emphasized, "You want to have clarity. To know for certain how everything will turn out. Still, the adventure is on the road of motion and discovery."

We'd like to avoid every misstep. However, it's like we're standing in a valley. When you start walking up the mountain, soon you'll be able to see new peaks (new choices), you could *not* see from the floor of the valley. Taking steps forward and upward, yields new clarity.

If in doubt, leave it out.

Still, you can protect yourself as you take action. For example, recently I received an email confirmation notice of an appointment with the president of an organization. I could respond by simply clicking "yes" (for "Yes, I am attending").

However, I saw that my name was misspelled. I had the thought, "If I send an email to correct this person's misspelling, it might bother her. It would be as if I'm criticizing her, and we have not even met yet."

So, I used my focus-point: "If in doubt, leave it out." I just clicked "yes" and left the idea of correcting the spelling of my name for during the in-person meeting.

In summary, to overcome procrastination (born of fear), "get strategic with it!" Use the process of S.P.A., so you can get in motion. Such action welcomes new opportunities.

Exercise #37: Write down your answer to:
How will you Preset the Trigger Sequence so you actually do your marketing efforts?

Pulling it All Together #2

Create Your *Three and Three Plan*

One of my mentors told me, "We underestimate the power of our environment: The people, stuff, routines and more of our daily life."

After that discussion, this idea arose in my mind:

Environment is a tyrant.

The solution is to *Create Your Own Environment.* How? I've guided my clients to create a **Three and Three Plan.**

In such a plan, you do two things:
a) Identify Three Marketing Categories/Projects
b) Identify Three "Smallest Actions to Start With"

This is where your progress begins.

(In the next section, I'll guide you to create an Accountability

Process.)

Exercise #38: Develop your *Three and Three Plan* as you write your answers to:

What three things do you want to focus on? Will it be one product with three forms of marketing?

Or do you want to start with three projects and add one *Smallest Action to Start With*—per each project?

Pulling it All Together #3

Create Your Accountability Process

How do you ensure that you get your marketing done each week? You set up an Accountability Process. With my clients, I use my *3 Levels/3 Forms of Goals — Strong Week Plan*.

This is a two-page form.

First, to give you an idea how this form works, I'll show you one that is filled in … on the next page:

****************Beginning of 2-Page Form****************
A Filled-In Example Below

3 Levels/3 Forms of Goals—Strong Week Plan.

Week of ____[date here]____
My goals for this week (my actions):

Levels:

Good:
2 marketing calls per day (5 days)

Excellent:
Complete my video that promotes my upcoming speech

Amazing:
Gain five other authors into my circle for cross-promotions

Now, tie in (write about) how the above Levels of Goals support your Goals for Your Blossoming 6-Months Journey:

Good
Bring in $10,000 with new online course

Excellent
Bring in $25,000 with new online course

Amazing
Bring in $100,000 with new online course and secure 6 major speaking engagements

As you do this, remember:
- Amazing happens with alliances.
- Motion brings clarity.

Also for this Week of _____

Write about Your 3 Forms of Goals:

Golden Pull Goals (vision)
Bring spouse and children to joyful vacation at Walt Disney World
Earn $200,000 per year — with things mostly automated

Dark Boot Goals (necessary and often needed to reduce/eliminate pain)
Reduce debt by 50%

Green Goals (*being*-related goals -- walk in nature, meditation, actions for your renewal)
Meditate for 5 minutes every morning
Take an afternoon walk outside every day

Well done, __[your name here]_!
Great to see your Using Structure to Blossom in Your Life

© Tom Marcoux Media, LLC   GetTheBigYES.com

[See the next page for a Blank copy of the form for your use.]

******************Beginning of 2-Page Form****************

3 Levels/3 Forms of Goals—Strong Week Plan.

Week of _____
My goals for this week (my actions):

Levels:

Good:

Excellent:

Amazing:

Now, tie in (write about) how the above Levels of Goals support your Goals for Your Blossoming 6-Months Journey:

Good

Excellent

Amazing

As you do this, remember:
- Amazing happens with alliances.
- Motion brings clarity.

Also for this Week of _____

Write about Your 3 Forms of Goals:

Golden Pull Goals (vision)

Dark Boot Goals (necessary and often needed to reduce/eliminate pain)

Green Goals (*being*-related goal—a walk in nature, meditation, actions for your renewal)

Well done, _____!
Great to see your Using Structure to Blossom in Your Life.

© Tom Marcoux Media, LLC   GetTheBigYES.com

Some Insights about Using the
3 Levels/3 Forms of Goals — Strong Week Plan.

You'll note that the form includes *3 Forms of Goals:*

Golden Pull Goals (vision)
These are the "shining goals" like "create a multi-million-dollar company that brightens people's lives."
[Some people try to only talk about the positive, shining goals. However, researchers have noted that people are *moved* by pain or eliminating pain which leads to ...]

Dark Boot Goals (necessary and often needed to reduce/eliminate pain)
A prime example of a Dark Boot Goal is for one to complete taxes paperwork. People in my audiences say that they only do taxes paperwork to avoid tax penalties. That's a powerful Dark Boot Goal.

Green Goals (*being*-related goals — walk in nature, meditation, actions for your renewal)
Green Goals are crucial because they keep you strong enough to move forward fast.

A Word about Using Progress Logs

A Progress Log can be a simple page in which you keep track of a pertinent piece of information. For example, I just noticed that at this moment, I have written 21,563 words of this book in your hands. I'll be adding more. Still, it's only Day 11 of my writing every day on this book.
An important detail: Keeping a Progress Log can

energize you to keep going because you see that you're successfully doing something good, and you can be proud of yourself for that.

Exercise #39: Begin your first efforts with using your notes about your End Game. Also fill out a *3 Levels/3 Forms of Goals—Strong Week Plan.* Place some form of Progress Log into your planner.

For example, I have a Progress Log (for this book in your hands) posted next to my computer monitor.

Tom Marcoux

Bonus Material

I first shared this material in an article I wrote entitled *Make Your Brand Irresistible – Get Clients!* ...

"If only the people I meet could really understand the value I bring to my clients," my new client, Sandra, said, deep concern in her eyes.

"I'm right there with you. I'll take you through a process; I call it **'Work it and trim it,'**" I began. "We're talking about using **Story** and making things **Brief** and **Compelling**."

a) *Story*
Novice business owners give people a list of what they do. Or they use an *Elevator Speech* that sounds like a commercial. **These things break rapport.** Instead, I guide my own clients to have a menu of stories that they can share. The story is what creates connection, and the story moves emotions.

Here's an example:

Wendy: "I'm curious. Do you have your own company or

do you work as part of a team?"

Cheryl: "I have my own company. We sell children's apparel online."

Wendy: "What inspired you to do that?"

Cheryl: (talks about how she was inspired by her three-year-old son).

Wendy: "Wow. You light up as you tell me all about that."

Cheryl: "Yeah. I still want to know what you do."

Wendy: "I help business owners like you invite people into their website. Recently, I helped a client, Irina, create a whole new homepage that gets people to click and dive into her website. She's now capturing many more new visitors. The improvement is 237%."

The above example is part of what I call an **Elevator Dialogue.**

My point is: Tell a well-crafted story. Make the emotional connection.

b) Brief

How do you know if what you're saying is brief enough?

Find out if the person can say it back to you.

Seven days ago, I got a phone call. "Tom, I think you'd be good to facilitate a marketing meeting at the company I work at. You *are* the Spoken Word Strategist."

Boom! My marketing was working.

Some time ago, I made the mistake of having a bunch of words under my name on my business card, including "CEO, Executive Coach, Author of 44 books …"

One of my own coaches pushed me. He said, "Why are you doing that?"

I replied, "I want to show that I'm different."

"Yeah, you're different. *But what counts is that people remember you,*" he said.

Many talented people find it hard to zero-in on the one thing that makes them great and different.

Ultimately, I learned that you keep testing things. When people can say something back to you, when they remember it, your marketing is working.

More does *not* mean better. *Memorable is better.*

c) Compelling

What is the pain that you alleviate for the client?

Where do they hurt?

Turn that into a Story of how you've helped a previous client. That's compelling.

One of my clients said this:

"Tom Marcoux helped me get more done in 10 days than other coaches in 2 years." – Brad Carlson, CEO, Mindstrong, LLC.

I've worked with CEOs and other business leaders. Where's the pain? Wasting time or other resources.

So, I help clients use leverage — small effort for BIG results

A Final Word and the Springboard to Your Dreams

Congratulations on your efforts with this book.

Please consider continuing to work with me through my **executive coaching** (phone and in-person), workshops and keynote addresses. Visit my blogs:

PitchPowerFest.com

GettheBigYES.com

StopBlockingtheAmazingYou.com

YourBodySoulandProsperity.com

Meanwhile, *to get even more value from this book*, take the plans and insights that you created and place them in some form in your calendar or day planner. *Plan and take action*. Return to these pages again and again to reconnect with the material and take your life to higher levels.

The best to you,

Tom

Tom Marcoux

Spoken Word Strategist

Executive Coach—Pitch Coach

Special Offer Just for Readers of this Book:

Contact Tom Marcoux at tomsupercoach@gmail.com for special discounts on **coaching,** books, workshops and presentations. Just mention your experience with this book.

Apply for a Free Consultation – see the video at TomSuperCoach.com/breakthrough

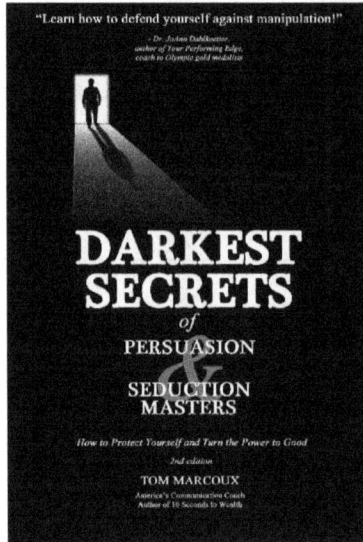

Excerpt from

Darkest Secrets of Persuasion and Seduction Masters: How to Protect Yourself and Turn the Power to Good

by Tom Marcoux, Executive Coach – Spoken Word Strategist
Copyright Tom Marcoux

. . . Now, I am in my 40's, with gray in my hair, and for 27 years I have been taking action to protect people.

And now is the time for me to protect you with the Countermeasures I reveal in this book.

Every human being needs to be able to break the trance that a Manipulator creates. You need to make good decisions so you are safe and you keep growing—and you are not cut down and crippled.

This Darkest Secrets material is so intense that I first released it only with the counterbalance of my most energizing and uplifting books, *Soar! Nothing Can Stop You This Year* and *Year of Awesome: How You Can Use 12 Success Principles including 10 Seconds to Wealth.*

An interviewer asked me: "Who can be the Manipulator?"

A co-worker, a boss, a salesperson, someone you're dating, and someone you think is a friend.

Now is the time—this very minute—for me to write this book to protect you.

I must speak the truth.

These Darkest Secrets of "persuasion masters" are ...

Wait a minute! Let's say it plainly: These are the Darkest Secrets of masters of manipulation. Throughout this book, I will call these people what they are: Manipulators.

Dictionary.com defines "manipulate" as "To influence or manage shrewdly or deviously.... To tamper with or falsify for personal gain."

In this book, we will look on a manipulator as one who deviously influences someone with no concern about that person's well-being, and who causes harm to that person.

Here is the first Darkest Secret:

Darkest Secret #1:
Manipulators Make You Hurt
and Then Offer the Salve.

Manipulators would invite you to go out in the sun for hours and then sell you the salve to soothe your burns. The problem is that we don't notice that this is what they're doing.

For example, you're considering the purchase of a house. A Manipulator asks the question, "So, where would you put your TV?" This question is designed to put you into a trance.

Dictionary.com defines "trance" as "a half-conscious state, seemingly between sleeping and waking, in which ability to function voluntarily may be suspended." Let's condense this: in a trance, you may not be able to function freely.

Here is the second Secret:

Darkest Secret #2:

Manipulators Put You into a Trance.

To protect yourself, you must learn to use Countermeasures to Break the Trance.

All the Countermeasures (actions you can take to break the trance) in this book will make you stronger and more capable of protecting yourself.

Now, we'll view the third Secret:

Darkest Secret #3:

Manipulators Care Nothing for You and Human Decency: They'll lie, cheat, and do whatever they need to do so they win—but their charm masks all this.

Let's return to the example of a Manipulator selling you a house. A Manipulator does not pause for an instant to see if you can truly afford the new house. The Manipulator would neglect to mention that you will not only have your mortgage payment of $900. There will be additional costs: home repairs, property tax, water, electricity, homeowner's insurance, and more. The Manipulator only emphasizes what he or she knows you want to hear: "Look! $900 is better than the $1500 you're paying for rent, which is just going down the toilet. And the $900 is an investment."

Let's go back to **Darkest Secret #1:**

Manipulators make you hurt and then offer the salve.

The Manipulator has you feeling good about the solution (salve) and feeling bad about your current life situation.

How? A Manipulator will make you hurt through questions such as:

• What bothers you about paying $1500 a month for rent? (The Manipulator will use a derisive tone when he says the word rent.)

• What is not smart about paying rent on someone else's house instead of investing in your own house?

• How do you feel about your children walking in the

neighborhood where you live now?

Do you see how these questions are designed to make you hurt enough so that you'll buy?

An interviewer asked me, "Tom, aren't these good arguments for purchasing a house?"

"What we're looking at is the *intention* of the influencer," I replied. "Let's look at our definition of a manipulator as one who deviously influences someone with no concern about that person's well-being, and who causes harm to that person. If the person truly cannot afford the house, he or she will be harmed by buying it. If the manipulator conceals the truth, the manipulator is doing harm. That's the important difference."

Some friends of mine are ethical and helpful real estate agents who truthfully reveal the whole situation and help the purchaser achieve her own goals.

In this book, we are talking about another type of person; that is, unethical Manipulators.

* * *

In any given moment, we need to remember the tactics Manipulators use. We will focus on the word D.A.R.K. so you can remember details easily and protect yourself from Manipulators.

D — Dangle something for nothing

A — Alert to scarcity

R — Reveal the Desperate Hot Button

K — Keep on pushing buttons

1. Dangle Something for Nothing

What do conmen and conwomen do to seize your attention? They make you think you're getting a "steal."

I recently saw a documentary in which a conman on a street in England showed a toy that looked like it was dancing. This fake product was actually dancing because of a hidden, invisible thread. The conman was dangling something for nothing. The Entranced Buyer thought he was getting something worth $20 for only $5. That was the trick. The Entranced Buyer felt that he was getting $15 extra of value for his $5. What the Buyer really got was something worth nothing. Similarly, I know someone who purchased a copy of a Disney movie from a street vendor in San Francisco. She brought the copy home and it was unwatchable—and the street vendor was never seen again.

An old phrase goes, "A conman cannot con someone who is not looking for something for nothing."

How to Protect Yourself from
"Dangle Something for Nothing"

Stop! Get on your cell phone and talk through the "deal" with someone you know who thinks clearly. Go home. Think about it. Do some research on the Internet. Listen to your gut feelings. If the salesman or conman is too insistent, get away from that Manipulator. Get quiet. Have a cup of water. Cool down. Break the Trance!

Break the Trance and Identify the Crucial Detail

Earlier, I mentioned that a Manipulator puts you into a trance. An added problem is that we put ourselves into a trance. For example, as you read this, are you thinking about your right toe? Most likely not (unless you stubbed your toe recently). The point is that we only focus on a tiny percentage of what is going on in our life.

Around fifteen years ago, I caused myself trouble because I put myself into a trance. I discovered that under certain conditions, friendship can make you nearly deaf. Here's how: I was producing a song for a motion picture. A good friend was singing backup in the chorus. Because of our friendship, I wanted him to sound great. I completely missed the Crucial Detail. In this kind of situation, the Crucial Detail is that what truly counts is how the lead singer sounds! I made a song that I could not release. What a waste of time and money! I had put myself into a trance.

In any situation in which the Manipulator is "dangling something for nothing," we often fall into a trance and miss the Crucial Detail. The most important detail is *not* that we're saving money if we order before midnight tonight. What counts is whether the product creates a lasting, crucial benefit in our lives. And is the benefit of the product worth the cost? Some people even program themselves to make mistakes by saying, "I can't pass up a bargain." The bargain is *not* the Crucial Detail.

Secrets to Break the Trance

This is the process of B.R.E.A.K.S. It will help you remember the proven methods to break a trance.

B — Breathe

R — Relax

E — Envision

A — Act on aromas

K — Keep moving

S — Smile

Secret #1: Breathe

Remember Secret #1: Manipulators make you hurt and then offer the salve. The Manipulator wants to put you into a state of being that fills you with a sense of urgency and anxiety. Oh, no! I'm going to miss the sale! Stop this highly vulnerable state. Take a deep breath.

End of Excerpt from *Darkest Secrets of Persuasion and*

Seduction Masters: How to Protect Yourself and Turn the Power to Good

Purchase your copy of this book (paperback or eBook) at online retailers

See **Free Chapters** of Tom Marcoux's 44 books at http://amzn.to/ZiCTRj

ABOUT THE AUTHOR

You want more and better, right? Imagine fulfilling your Big Dream.

Tom Marcoux can help you—in that he's coached thousands of people: CEOs, small business leaders, graduate students (at Stanford University) speakers, and authors.

Tom is known as an effective **Executive Coach** and **Spoken Word Strategist**.

(and Thought Leader—okay, writing 44 books helped with that!)

** *CEOs, Vice-Presidents, Other Executives, Small Business Leaders:*

You know that leading people and speaking at your best can be tough.

Tom solves problems while helping you amplify *your own Charisma, Confidence, and Control of Time.*

"Tom Marcoux coached me to get more done in 10 days than other coaches in 2 years."
– Brad Carlson, CEO of MindStrong LLC

Interested? Email Tom at tomsupercoach@gmail.com Ask for a Special Report: "9 Deadly Mistakes to Avoid for Your Next Speech."

You've heard that you need to tell YOUR STORY well, right? (We're talking about brand, product, or profile for a

job.)

The San Francisco Examiner designated Tom Marcoux as "The Personal Branding Instructor." Why? Tom has helped thousands of clients, audiences, MBA students express their own **powerful Personal Brand.** Tom helps **you communicate powerfully so people trust you** and gain what you're offering (product, service, an idea!).

As a **Pitch Coach,** Marcoux is an expert on STORY. He won a Special Award at the EMMY AWARDS, and he directed a feature film that went to the CANNES FILM MARKET and earned international distribution. Tom founded PitchPowerFest.com (Also see GetTheBigYES.com)

You need to give a great Speech. How about a TED Talk?

"Tom Marcoux has coached me to make my speeches compelling and powerful. He's helping me prepare my TED Talk. Do your career a big favor and engage **Tom Marcoux, the Spoken Word Strategist.**" – Dr. JoAnn Dahlkoetter, author of *Your Performing Edge* and Coach to CEOs and Olympic Gold Medalists

"Tom helped me unearth deeply emotional and humorous moments in my speech to move the hearts of the audience. He was there for me unconditionally. He went above and beyond anything that I expected. During every interaction that I had with Tom, I felt that I learnt something profound.

I highly recommend for anyone who wants to give a great speech that you work with Tom Marcoux as your Speech Coach and Spoken Word Strategist." – Krishna Noru

As a CEO, Tom leads teams in the United Kingdom, India and the USA. Tom guides clients and audiences (LinkedIn, IBM, Sun Microsystems, etc.) in "Soar with Confidence", leadership, team-building, power time management and branding.

> "Tom Marcoux has been an NAB Conference favorite [speaker] for six years. And he is very energetic." – John Marino, Vice President, National Association of Broadcasters, Washington, D.C.

One of Tom's *Darkest Secrets* books rose to **#1 on Amazon.com Hot New Releases in Business Life** (and in Business Communication). A member of the National Speakers Association for over 16 years, Tom is a professional coach and guest expert on TV, radio, and print.

Tom addressed National Association of Broadcasters' Conference six years in a row. With a degree in psychology, he has presented as a guest lecturer at Stanford University, DeAnza College, and California State University. Over the years, Tom has taught business communication, designing careers, public speaking, science fiction cinema/literature and comparative religion at Academy of Art University. He is engaged in book/film projects *Crystal Pegasus* (children's graphic novel) and *Jack AngelSword* (thriller-fantasy).

This is YOUR OPPORTUNITY. Apply for a <u>Free Strategy Session</u> with Tom Marcoux at tomsupercoach.com/breakthrough. See the Video.

Tom Marcoux says, "Because of my unique coaching methods, I emphasize with my clients: **You will achieve more than you believe.**"

provides *A.C.T. Coaching* (Assess, Create, Trim) and

T.O.P. Coaching (Transform, Optimize, Power-communicate).

With his unique background as a trained feature film director, actor and screenwriter, Tom will role-play with you so you're ready for the tough meeting and even tougher speech or sales presentation.

> "Using just one of Tom Marcoux's methods, I got more done in 2 weeks than in 6 months." – Jaclyn Freitas, M.A.

Consider Tom Marcoux's well-received Online Course **Get the Big YES: Use Extreme Confidence to Get Clients and Get It Done!** ... send an email to TomSuperCoach@gmail.com

Become a fan of Tom's graphic novels/feature films:

- Fantasy Thriller: *Jack AngelSword*
  type "JackAngelSword" at Facebook.com

- Urban Fantasy: *Jenalee Storm*
  At Facebook.com type: "JenaleeStorm"

- Science fiction: *TimePulse*
  www.facebook.com/timepulsegraphicnovel

- Children's Fantasy: *Crystal Pegasus*
  www.facebook.com/crystalpegasusandrose

See **Free Chapters** of Tom Marcoux's 44 books—visible at online retailers.